BRITISH PRIMITIVE FANTASISTS

A Survey of Portal Painters

BRITISH PRIMITIVE FANTASISTS

A Survey of Portal Painters

ERIC LISTER

ALPINE FINE ARTS COLLECTION, LTD.

Publishers of Fine Art Books, New York

Published in 1982 by:
ALPINE FINE ARTS COLLECTION, LTD.
164 Madison Avenue, New York, New York 10016

ISBN: 0-933516-53-3

Design: Philip Grushkin

Editor: Matthew Slatin

This book was produced in Belgium by Offset Printing Van den Bossche ▣

Contents

To my partner, Lionel Levy, who has tolerated me for the past twenty-two years, and who, for the past twelve months, has not been able to have the use of a typist, a telephone, a chair or a pen when he most needed one.

ACKNOWLEDGMENTS

I would like to extend my sincere thanks for the assistance of:

Sally Pasmore, Ron McCrindle, Tony Ashbee, Martin Leman, David Carter, Kenneth Balfour, Mr. & Mrs. H. Campling, Harry Leuckart and Jean Muir, Mr. & Mrs. C. Arrowsmith and Mr. & Mrs. Eliot Kastner for loaning paintings from their collections, thus enabling me to select the best examples from each artist's work.

Andreas Kalman, stalwart curmudgeon of the London art world and owner of the excellent Crane Kalman Gallery—may all your serves be aces.

Ruth Nathan in New York for her invaluable assistance in getting this project off the ground.

My colleague and friend, Jess Wilder, for her infinite patience.

All the artists featured in this book, thank you for your friendly cooperation.

Photographers: Bill Toomey, Michael Todd-White, Atlas Photography Ltd., Walter Dorin and The Camera Press.

Peter Vigurs, Keeper of Fine Art at the City Museum and Art Gallery, Stoke-on-Trent, for his research on the work of C. W. Brown.

Peter Blake for his assistance with the work of Ted Wilcox.

I would also like to thank friends and clients too numerous to name, who have unknowingly contributed, through gallery photographs of the original paintings in their collections.

Introduction

The function of a label is identification; without a label, identification relies on expertise or chance. The label "primitive/naive" is firmly attached to the contemporary artist working in this style; this is unfortunate because it has become a complete misnomer in the last quarter of the twentieth century. How many primitive people remain? A few tribes in New Guinea or the remoter areas of the South American jungle? A few Kurdish and African communities, sought after and "discovered" by documentary film makers? Certainly no one now living in Britain, Europe or America can be described as "primitive." However, many people today could be described as at least somewhat "naive."

Interestingly enough, these two characteristics, one quite common, the other extremely rare, can produce a remarkable awareness and perception when directed towards creative art. It is not merely coincidental that these mature artists have a somewhat childlike vision. The art of children is direct and uncluttered; the difference is that the child's artistic vision changes drastically as the child grows older, whereas the naive artist's vision often remains frozen from mid-childhood. This does not necessarily apply to the naive's technique which can be as sophisticated as that of the best academically trained artist. It is in their mind's picture that their finished work differentiates from that of normal academics.

The primitive is totally lacking in sophistication. The difference between primitive and naive can be seen within the art, not necessarily within the artist. This is a very fine line, which up until now has caused much confusion in its definition. This line does not concern the individual, only an artistic style labelled "primitive" or "naive." The subject matter, perspective and style of this self-motivated naive art has an underlying obsession which relates it to the established primitive.

Prior to the 1940's, African wood carvers did not produce masks or figures for decoration. To them, the concept of an ornament was completely alien. These objects were produced only for functional and ritualistic purposes. The craftsman failed to understand the concept of art for art's sake. After the Second World War these craftsmen began to realise the commercial value of their work as mere objects, and it is from this time that the quality of their works distinctly deteriorates and the carver, who was once regarded by his tribe in as high esteem as the witch doctor, and whose work was often considered to be sacred, soon lost the respect of the community. No doubt his recently acquired riches compensated somewhat for his loss of status.

Early in the 1900's sophisticated artists such as Derain, Picasso, Matisse and latterly Epstein and Moore recognised the importance of these ethnic objects as works of art. These European artists attempted to incorporate such a primitive quality in their own work. They were of course intellectuals producing work specifically for an art market, quite the opposite of the African or Oceanic craftsmen who carved instinctively and obsessively, injecting their objects with "soul."

A vital part of early man's communication are the superb cave paintings, now revered as "art." However, after millions of years, they still serve as a communication link with primitive man. In a sense, their function today is as important as it ever was. The commercial artists working between the 17th and 19th centuries produced shop and tavern signs, functional objects to which they added decorative touches of their own. These painted signs were an important means of communication to a mainly illiterate and unsophisticated public. Today, this form of communication has largely been superceded by widespread literacy and the use of the camera. Ironically, since the advent of the European Economic Community and international trade, a symbol sign has once again made an appearance as a simple solution to the language barrier. Nowadays, the graphic designer creates an important link within the community, as did the artist in the past.

Traces of nineteenth century functional communication still existed until quite recently. Some of the less sophisticated artists that appear in this book, such as A. W. Chesher, Alfred Wallis, James Lloyd, Ralph Crossley, James Dixon, C. W. Brown and George Kirk (all no longer living), were simple, honest and the last of a line of British primitive artists whose main purpose was one of expression, before any thought of exhibition or sale. Contemporary naive artists are often sophisticated individuals; some with a minimal amount of art tuition and others fully trained. Their art is often obsessive but produced with a commercial eye, decorative and non-functional. This is in no way meant to decry the modern naive artists whose work is as valid as their predecessors. In this "media-controlled" world they are less of a necessity and more of a luxury. With increased quality in materials and highly developed skills, some of these artists produce work that is on a par with some of the finest trained artists. The difference is an esoteric one and amounts to an almost indefinable quality of vision. It is important to look at as many paintings as possible to develop an eye for the genuinely naive. Do not be put off by craftsmanship; many contemporary naives are superb technicians, but somewhere within these paintings an almost childlike quality can be identified.

As African carving has gradually deteriorated since its "discovery," likewise most of the naive artists in Yugoslavia, Bali, Haiti, Brazil, etc. are now catering to the tourist trade. Buyers arrive with the preconceived idea that naive art is a sugary concoction of charming characters who inhabit a "Walt Disney" world. Paradoxically, some of the finest naive art comes from the most sophisticated countries. Naive British artists have been virtually overlooked abroad. However, largely due to an inherent British eccentricity, they are among some of the finest to be found. Their art tends to be less sweet and more fantastic than the better known naives of the Continent.

The late James Lloyd, an artist of the highest calibre, can be considered alongside any of the world's best 20th century primitives including Frenchmen Le Douanier Rousseau and Camille Bombois and American artists like Morris Hirschfield or Horace Pippin.

During the many years I have been connected with naive and primitive Art I have been repeatedly asked to define the labels. It is still not easy to give an entirely satisfactory explanation, but to put it at its most succinct, I would say that primitive painting is unsophisticated art by an unsophisticated artist, naive art is unsophisticated art by a sophisticated artist, and that both are linked by obsession.

It is because of this inability to clearly define the primitive/naive label that it has become necessary in my opinion to drop both terms, except where the specific artist can be quite clearly defined, and adopt the description "self-taught," enabling us to encompass the entire spectrum from the unsophisticated primitive to the sophisticated naive and all the other variations. There is the additional fact that 90% of the artists featured have exhibited at the Portal Gallery, and this of course justifies the overall group description of "Portal Painters."

Self-taught can, in a sense, mean an artist who has re-educated himself or re-emerged, and has forsaken his or her art education to paint in a free and unencumbered manner (see biographies of Irvine Peacock or Reginald Pepper as definitive examples). One can thus understand what might otherwise appear to be a contradiction in terms.

It is difficult to estimate the number of known, good, self-taught painters in Britain today, but my own guess would be around 150. It would therefore be impractical for me to attempt to include more than a selection in this book. With this selection I have perhaps indulged in my own somewhat bizarre taste. My regret is that I cannot include so many more of the excellent artists I know of. There is always a space problem. Perhaps two volumes will be necessary. That is a thought. . . .

ERIC LISTER
January 1982
London

Portal Gallery

Fellow jazz enthusiasts were scarce in the Lancashire seaside town of
Southport during the summer of 1942. I had heard through a friend that
a boy named Arthur Davidson was a jazz fan, so I duly visited him. I
found him and another boy rolling about on the lawn of a rambling
Victorian house, waving their arms around in mirth during a giggling fit
over some obscure and private piece of imagination. When this duo had
simmered down somewhat, I found out that Arthur was the shorter lad
and that his pal was Lionel Levy. It is now almost forty years since that
summer's day in Southport, but these two spotty-faced youths, now
middle aged men, can still be seen (suitably esconced in leather armchairs)
giggling uncontrollably over the same piece of esoteric, imaginary nonsense.

   Arthur, Lionel and I chummed up from the start. Jazz record sessions,
wrestling, and chasing chicks at the local Habonim club were our most
serious occupations. From '43–'46, Arthur and I became shipmates in the
Merchant Navy. I saw a little action and completed forty-nine Atlantic
crossings, mostly on great liners like the Queen Mary or the Mauritania,
ferrying troops. When berthed in New York, during every spare evening
we had, Arthur and I enjoyed hearing and meeting most of the leading
American jazz musicians on the now legendary 52nd Street. I actually
got to sit in with some of the greats and claim to be the only British jazz
musician to have sat with such diverse personalities as Bunk Johnson and
Charlie Parker during the postwar years. Our friendship and mutual
sense of the ridiculous continued after the war when Arthur, Lionel and

Eric were well-known characters in Southport and nearby Liverpool.

I moved to London in 1956, became involved in car racing, vintage car sales and of course jazz, but I kept in touch with my old friends, and when Lionel came down for a weekend, early in 1959, we discussed the possibility of starting an art gallery, Lionel had some art school experience and I had become interested in primitive art, after collecting English Staffordshire pottery with its modelled and highly coloured images.

On Lionel's return to Liverpool, I began the search for suitable premises in which to open a gallery. Even in those days, prime position shop property in London was hard to find, so it was not for several months until Lionel and I came across a florist's shop in Mayfair with distinct possibilities. Because of its small size, and the fact that the basement housed a busy barber shop (on a long lease), we managed to buy our section at a reasonable price, considering the fact that we were located in one of the world's finest areas for the sale of objets d'art.

What we lacked in experience we made up for in enthusiasm. With the help of a few friends like the Campbells, we opened the Portal Gallery in December, 1959. Our choice of the name came from *Roget's Thesaurus*, where it is defined as a symbol for opening. It was our original intention to specialise in the works of northern artists, a policy which still exists to a lesser degree today. Although we had stated our policy in *Art News*, we were initially unable to find more than a couple of artists from the north of England, so, armed with a libary book entitled *Promising Artists of 1956*, we began seeking artists by knocking on studio doors. In retrospect we must compliment ourselves on our inexperienced but natural good taste; this almost indefinable quality has been our most important asset in twenty-two years as art dealers. Amongst our early exhibitors were some of Britian's most celebrated contemporary artists; Peter Blake, Joe Tilson, Michael Fussell and Patrick Hughes.

As Lionel continued living in Liverpool, I ran the gallery myself until 1963, depending on girlfriends to bring in my sandwiches and coffee. It was during those formative years that we defined our present policy. Lionel knew a Liverpool artist, George Wallace Jardine, who was our first fantasy painter. His highly detailed and delicate compositions were favoured by our early clients. Gradually, our scruffy little gallery with the odd couple—smiling Lionel and glowering Eric—was being discovered by discerning patrons. Although we did not realise it then, our business timing was excellent, coinciding with the beginning of the "pop" era, a rapid rise in affluence and a revival in the Victorian pastime of collecting. Actors, musicians, designers, writers and photographers, many of whom are now household names like: Julie Christie; Michael Caine; Rod Steiger; David Niven; David Bailey; The Beatles, particularly Ringo Starr and their manager Brian Epstein; Ionesco; Vincent Price; Robert Morley; Samuel Beckett; John Mills; Kim Novak; and many others, were amongst our earliest visitors and have remained friends. Almost from the beginning, the word got around among artists that we were a friendly gallery (you've got to understand Eric though) and they called in, as we are convenient for the Cork Street art circuit. People still ask where we find our artists, and the answer still applies—they find us.

Publicity was forthcoming from the beginning; newspapers, TV and radio enjoy stories about self-taught artists and by 1963 we had amassed the best stable in Britain—James Lloyd, Bernard Carter, Neil Davenport, A. W. Chesher, and fantasy painters Jardine, Belasco and Cornelia Dibble—an amalgam of artists who were already recognised as the "Portal School." By 1963, Lionel had moved to London permanently and apart from our cramped accommodation (we were sometimes known as the Porthole Gallery or the Packing Case Gallery). There was the nuisance of an hysterical barber beneath us who once attacked me with a razor for erecting a barrier between our gallery and his shop, to avoid confusion amongst our respective clients. No doubt the most important landmark in establishing us as a primitive gallery was the 1964 BBC TV film, *The Dotty World of James Lloyd*.

By this time we were affluent enough to buy a typewriter and employ a 'man Friday' typist, install a second telephone and build a minute and perilous glass-fronted contraption overlooking the gallery, which we cynically referred to as our office. We were almost as cramped as if in a rush hour subway and had no privacy whatsoever, which caused a great deal of bickering between Lionel and the current secretary. During the mid-sixties, a petite, good-looking girl named Kerry Bate joined us and soon became a dominant force in quietening us down, or occasionally rising above us to put one of us down. We of course made her our third director to keep all our quarrels in the family. All of this helped to keep our customers amused most of the time, and if they didn't like the paintings at least they enjoyed the entertainment. Conversely, there have been many occasions when these clients have been a source of entertainment to us.

One afternoon, an elderly English "beanpole," wearing a faded tweed cape, deerstalker hat and highly polished, ancient cracked leather boots, vaguely wandered in. In a modulated and very British tone he immediately asked me the price of the very first picture on the wall by the entrance. He seemed unconcerned with the artist or subject of the painting, and on hearing the price, plunged his hands into his various pockets. He pulled out bank notes of several denominations which fluttered to the carpet. I picked them up and helped him count out the required amount, whereupon he sauntered out of the gallery to walk down Grafton Street. I ran after him, asking for his name and where to send a receipt and deliver the painting. He looked at me as if we had never met, said, "That's quite alright," and walked away. I put him down as another nut, not to be confused with the man in the tan raincoat who had exposed himself to Kerry during the previous week.

About two years after the old codger had left us the money and the picture, and long after Lionel and I had decided that we could do with a few more customers like him, a large and ancient Daimler pulled up outside and a withered, begaitered chauffeur came in to mumble something about a painting for Sir Blenkinsop Carruthers. None of us had heard of such a gentleman and, as the old retainer had no idea which painting he was supposed to collect, we were all rather bemused. I finally remembered the vague and nutty old gentleman from two years ago and, on describing him to the chauffeur and verifying the fact that he was rather absent-minded, we scrabbled around in our cramped store cupboard and handed him the appropriate painting. To fully satisfy my curiosity I asked the chauffeur if Sir Blenkinsop was in the habit of buying goods and not collecting them for years. The reply was, "Oh, he probably imagined he bought it yesterday, sir."

A complete variety of people parade through the gallery daily, from all walks of life and probably from every civilised country in the world. A high percentage of Portal's overseas clients are from the U.S.A. with Holland, Germany and Switzerland also predominant. One gets used to their characteristics and deals accordingly. A built-in knowledge of psychology is a must. Very few people are difficult to deal with and although we regularly trust clients with paintings on approval and extended payments, it is an extremely rare occasion when anyone lets us down.

During the so-called "swinging sixties" in London, Portal's large

Edwardian window became famous for its offbeat displays. We had always maintained that humour was an integral part of art, as art is an integral part of life, not to be taken too seriously. Our window displayed surrealistic objects by Bruce Lacey, or perhaps a Victorian Penny Farthing Bicycle, or at Christmas, a display of Sam Smith's clever wood "mood indicators," a kind of paddle stick with beautifully painted faces on either side with one happy expression "Yes" and one grumpy expression "No," (Lionel and me perhaps?), satirical humour based on the faded glories of the British Empire.

At this juncture, around 1964/5, the media picked up on the Portal Gallery. We were beginning to enjoy the fruits of extensive publicity. Several BBC and ITV television films about our artists and full colour covers on Sunday supplements and magazines came our way. Some art critics still avoided us, as they didn't seem to be able to give credit to unsophisticated paintings, even of the finest quality. Our gallery artists lacked the esoteric mystique which most critics require to be able to write their self-indulgent and often uncomprehensible articles. Although this irritated us somewhat at the time, as the years pass we have realised that few people pay any attention to the British art critics on their home ground. People do pay attention, however, to major articles in the colour supplements and on television, as proven by the popularity of our artists. Even our own individual personalities have been identified by the media—expansive Lionel and curmudgeon Eric.

I began my extensive travels and search for ethnic art around 1963, across the U.S. by Greyhound and three months in Mexico and Guatemala. The following year, a six week trip across Europe, Scandinavia and Russia, again by bus. I love road trips; I meet interesting people and enjoy the leisurely pace. Travelling by road to India in 1966 was a great adventure and my search for antique cars with the ubiquitous John Warth is material for a novel. Trips across Africa, South America, the Far East, China and Japan followed, with many adventures and misadventures. One such jaunt came about through my meeting in the gallery during the mid-sixties, an almost legendary hero of mine, the American writer and humourist, S. J. Perelman. We became close friends, travelled together and eventually embarked on a planned trip overland (sponsored by *The Sunday Times*) from Paris to Peking in Sid's 1949 MG open touring car. We were joined on this insane jaunt by a certain Mr. Beer whose life's work had been spent on the study and maintenance of MG's. The only thing that didn't go wrong was the aged car. After a four month nightmarish journey through fifteen countries, narrowly avoiding earthquakes, coup d'états, floods and famine, we finally made it to the Chinese border, with tempers frayed, stomachs ruined and nerves shattered.

During the early seventies, some of our veteran artists, like the prestigious James Lloyd whose work now hangs in the Tate Gallery, A. W. Chesher and James Dixon, died. However, from time to time we do manage to collect enough work of these deceased artists to put on a show; for example, the successful James Lloyd retrospective at the Camden Art Centre in 1977. We are planning another Lloyd show during 1982/3. New artists, like Kit Williams, Beryl Cook, P. J. Crook, Fergus Hall, and many more, joined us as the gallery took on a stronger flavour of fantasy alongside the primitive. People tend to associate us more with the naives than the fantasists, but we have always favoured both styles, even showing the celebrated Belgian surrealist, Magritte, during the early sixties. Now our descriptive "self-taught" covers the entire field between the primitive, sophisticated realist and fantasy artists. By 1975, when our current "third man," Jess Wilder, joined us (Kerry Bate had had enough and left to become a talented book binder), we finally got rid of our monkey-like barber and doubled the gallery's space by converting the basement and removing the "aviary" we called an office. Now we continue our squabbles as to who should sit behind the desk, as we only have three chairs. Our junior, nicknamed "The Nipper" has to stand up permanently unless one of us is at lunch. The enhancement of our premises has meant we can carry two exhibitions simultaneously, with the obvious beneficial results. During the mid-seventies our Christmas exhibitions featured a group of some seventy Portal artists, each painting their own version of a theme such as "Noah's Ark," "Adam and Eve," or "Jonah and the Whale." The 1981 "Great Portal Pig Extravaganza" is a fascinating and amusing exercise in personal renditions on a pig theme. If anyone asks me why the Portal Gallery has become something of a fondly regarded London institution, the answer is in four parts: Personal attention to clients and artists alike—we are always available to look at new work; Intimacy—we never get too large; Improvisation—people generally dislike formality; The business "marriage" of Lionel and me which has survived due to our mutual sense of humour and the ridiculous—nothing in business can be that serious.

PORTAL PAINTERS

A Survey of British Primitive Fantasists

I

Neil Davenport

Neil Davenport was in his teens during the late 1920's and a pupil at Malborough (one of the better known English public schools, where, incidentally his father was bursar) and became fascinated by the more magnificent motor cars of the era. No humble Ford, Austin, Citroen or Fiat for young Neil, he only dreamt about the superb and the exotic— Rolls Royces, Bugattis, Dusenbergs, Hispano-Suizas and Isotta Franchinis purring along the *Promenade des Anglais* at Nice or along the driveway of an elegant English country mansion or speeding down a twisting Alpine road with a nondescript black sedan in close pursuit. These magnificent automobiles were usually driven by a young, handsome, uniformed chauffeur, whilst the Lord and Lady or Count and Countess were luxuriating in the deeply cushioned rear compartment.

One day, after he wrote (in his impeccable handwriting) to Rolls Royce asking for catalogues and literature on their latest Phantom Laudaulette limousine, Neil's imagination became a reality. Obviously the Rolls people were very impressed with the letter and posh address, because one afternoon Neil was called from class to meet a gentleman who, to Neil's amazement, turned out to be a representative of Rolls Royce. He was standing beside the gleaming limousine he had enquired about. When the gentleman realised his mistake and saw that his prospect wasn't even old enough to drive, he took it in good spirit and invited Neil and a group of his chums for a joy ride around the countryside. Neil later gave up a successful career as a photographer to become an artist, teaching himself to paint during the immediate post-war years. With a photographer's eye for composition and a natural and lively sense of colour, he developed a very fresh and naive style of painting.

What makes Neil Davenport's style so recognisable is the subject matter which has remained unchanged since he started painting—his youthful fantasies have matured into paintings. They are truly nostalgic, based on his travels through Europe as a young man, together with a taste for the novelists of the period, Michael Arlen, W. Somerset Maugham,

NEIL DAVENPORT
Tea on the Lawn.
Oil/canvas, 20″ × 16″, 1973

P. G. Wodehouse, and chronicler of the Jazz Age, F. Scott Fitzgerald. Neil Davenport has created a world of memories and imagination with his own brand of humour. The wonderful motor cars, now mostly in collections, can be seen in their natural habitat, the atmosphere of the twenties and thirties—the European spas which were once the play-grounds of the royal and aristocratic families of countries which no longer exist, or Ruritanian retreats which often became the victims of coup d'états, hence the scenes in Davenport's paintings of Rolls or Hispanos laden with the family heirlooms crashing through customs posts amidst a hail of bullets. In calmer times the beautiful countess' secret tryst with her

NEIL DAVENPORT
Hotel Regina.
Oil/canvas, 20″ × 16″, 1978

chauffeur while her elderly husband is playing the tables at the casino. Jolly parties on the Côte d'Azur, or the eccentric British aristocracy picnicing on the grounds of their castle, ignoring the fact that the west wing is blazing away, attended by the local fire brigade who are gallantly rescuing the young housemaid. The Grand Duchess, oblivious to the fact that, through a certain financial embarrassment, she is forced to leave her magnificent chateau and move to a less ostentatious abode, nevertheless is suddenly inspired to give him an impromtu performance accompanied by her handsome live-in chauffeur!

NEIL DAVENPORT
Swansong.
Oil/canvas, 20″ × 16″

26

II
Alfred Wallis

Alfred Wallis and James Lloyd undoubtedly share the distinction of being the two British primitive painters most accepted by the art Establishment. They both have works in the Tate Gallery and Wallis has even had a one-man exhibition there. His work also has the distinction of being in the collection of the Museum of Modern Art, New York. I am confident that his compatriot, James Lloyd, given time, will receive as much acclaim (the art Establishment moves like a snail under sedation). What these two artists had in common was the rare gift of originality, which in these cases is synonymous with quality.

Alfred Wallis was born in 1855 in Devonport, close to Plymouth, Devon. His mother was a native of the offshore Scilly Islands. The family was poor, and his father worked as a master paver. His mother died when Alfred was very young, and at the tender age of nine, he left home and went to sea as a cabin boy. For several years he worked on fishing vessels on the Atlantic trading route with Newfoundland and worked the Grand Banks. Some sources attempt to discredit this early period of his life, claiming it was imagination, but I feel (as an ex-sailor myself) that his observation of the ocean and the horizon, and his almost abstract depiction of the steam and sailing vessels in which he sailed, suggests very strongly that the sea must have played a major part in his life, and was the obvious inspiration for his paintings.

At the age of 20, Alfred Wallis married Susan Ward, a widow twenty-one years his senior, and reputedly the mother of seventeen

children. Alfred soon added two more to her brood, although they both died in infancy. A decidedly odd couple, Alfred a boyish twenty, barely over five feet tall, and now the step-father of Susan's children, he was hardly distinguishable from the other youngsters. They had set up home in Penzance and, to enable him to spend more time with his recently acquired and enormous family, he gave up deep-sea fishing and worked locally and around the English east and west coasts fishing for pilchards, herrings and mackerel.

It was not until 1890, when he was thirty-five, that he quit fishing and moved across the Penwith Peninsula to St. Ives where he was to spend the rest of his life. He set up a business of his own in St. Ives as a marine junk dealer buying and selling scrap iron and second hand fishing gear. This gained him the local nickname, "Old Iron." He made a reasonable living up to the beginning of the First World War, when the Cornish fishing industry began to decline. His rag and bone junk business closed down and he and his now elderly wife (the children had left for more lucrative pastures) moved into a tiny fisherman's cottage they bought with what remained of his life's savings. From that time onwards he barely scraped a living as an odd job man and by selling his home-made ice cream to the few tourists in the vicinity. He became increasingly obsessed with religion and read only the bible and old local newspapers. Susan and Alfred became more and more withdrawn and isolated from the community. He was regarded by many locals as a "bit daft" and was often teased by their children.

In 1922, Susan died and left Alfred entirely alone to struggle on

ALFRED WALLIS
Penzance Harbour.

miserably. He was suspicious of strangers, independent and quite stubborn. At the age of seventy, he received his old age pension. This pittance helped to improve his lot for a while, so with the help of a few neighbors, Wallis survived. Two of these friends, Mr. Armour, an antique dealer, and his neighbor, Mr. Edwards, the watchmaker, helped Alfred Wallis in his efforts to become an artist. In an early and now rare book on Wallis by Sven Berlin (published in 1949), Berlin describes how Wallis, one day in 1925 told Edwards how he felt like "doin' a bit of paintin' to pass away time." Before then, Wallis, according to his step-grandson Jacob Ward, had done some pencil drawings on scraps of paper, much to the amusement of his wife, but he had never used paint and a brush before. Apparently he found a couple of cheap brushes and with some odd pots of house paint he painted a few pictures of boats on pieces of cardboard. He showed these to Armour and Edwards, asking with pride "What do 'ee think on they?" Both his friends nodded their approval and encouraged him to carry on painting.

Old Alfred continued painting and like many other primitives became obsessed by his own work. He was really only happy when painting pictures of boats, the local fishing grounds, schooners, steamers, fish, harbours and occasionally strange aerial views of St. Ives. He began by using glossy ship's enamel paint, working on scraps of wood and boxes of all shapes and sizes, signing them "Alfred Wallis" or "A. Wallis," in a childlike hand, but he never dated them. Sometimes he worked with great haste and forgot to sign them at all, but his work is so distinctive, fresh and alive it needs no signature. His compositions were always right, no matter how childish they looked to the untrained eye.

His depth of colour and the abstract way in which he painted the sea was immediately recognised by the leading British artists, Christopher Wood and Ben Nicholson, who were living and working nearby in 1928. They happened to pass by the old man's cottage one day and through the open door they saw him painting, surrounded by his work, nailed to the walls and back of the door. The texture of the boards which he used made the original surface part of the picture, and the strong, but limited, selection of marine greys, blacks, rich greens, dark blues and whites, were a revelation to the two artists, both of whose later paintings are obviously influenced by this unsophisticated old man. They befriended Wallis who was flattered by their attention, and proudly sold them several paintings for a few shillings each, which would have seemed quite fair in those days.

Nicholson and Wood soon introduced his work to their friends in
London, who in turn were captivated by its strange and simple quality.
Some of his most ardent collectors were artists and scholars—H. S. Ede,
Adrian Stokes, Barbara Hepworth, Winifred Nicholson and Herbert

ALFRED WALLIS
Voyage to Labrador.

Read, who all visited Wallis in Cornwall during the next few years. Although he was admired by this rather select group of art sophisticates, however, they kept Wallis to themselves. Consequently, his prices never rose. However, his financial problems and, even more importantly, his loneliness, were alleviated for a few years.

Alfred Wallis was happy to talk about his paintings as if they were living experiences. They showed his contempt for houses and his love of ships. He would punctuate his conversations with quotations from the bible and his homespun philosophy, his conversations often being as colourful as his paintings.

ALFRED WALLIS
The Hold House
Port Mear Square Island,
Port Mear Beach.

During the 1930's his reputation grew slowly and, due to his artist friends, his work eventually appeared at both Tooth's Gallery in London and the Wertheim Gallery. Ben Nicholson presented one of his works to New York's Museum of Modern Art, whilst several could be seen hanging in H. S. Ede's office at the Tate Gallery, London.

Like so many artists, and probably due to his age, his work began to decline somewhat during the late thirties. His almost classical simplicity, a feature of the earlier work, disappeared and the paintings became more cluttered, almost as if he was rushing to say all he could about the sea before he died. At the end of the decade and with the advent of World War II, Wallis gradually grew weaker and, with very few friends at hand, the end of his life was tragic. He had always dreaded ending his days in the workhouse but he was taken to the Madrau Institution despite efforts made by his artist friends. The war had made it unavoidable. He carried on painting for a while and, although he was thought slightly mad by the derelict inmates, he was respected by the staff as someone rather special, a very old man with long flowing white hair—a prophet and an artist.

Alfred Wallis died in August, 1942, aged 87, and at his own request was given a Salvation Army funeral. This was attended by the few of his friends who were not away fighting in the war.

On his grave at Porthmear Cemetery, St. Ives, which was paid for by these artist friends, there is a slab decorated with tiles by Master Potter, Bernard Leach. They depict a lighthouse with steps leading down to a stormy sea. Climbing these steps is a small old man holding a cane. On the grave are the words: Alfred Wallis, Artist and Mariner.

BIBLIOGRAPHY:

Alfred Wallis, Cornish Primitive Painter by Edwin Mullins.
Alfred Wallis Exhibition Catalogue, Waddington Galleries, London, 1965.
Alfred Wallis Arts Council Exhibition, Tate Gallery, May-June, 1968.

I I I

Ralph Crossley

Ralph Crossley, a Yorkshireman, was born in 1884 in the tiny hamlet of Crigglestone. He was one of a family of ten. As a young man he became a bricklayer's apprentice and in fact remained a "brickie" for all his working life.

Crossley married and moved to a village outside the north Lancashire industrial town of Preston, where he spent the rest of his life, outliving his wife by twenty years and dying at the age of eighty-two in 1966. Very little is known about Ralph Crossley and his life story has been pieced together by short conversations with people who remembered him. It appears that he was happily married, although a somewhat eccentric and extremely intense person. After his wife's death his eccentricities extended to his begging for money from neighbours and strangers, even though his wages as a 'brickie' were quite adequate.

It is not known exactly when he started to paint, but it seems to have been during the late thirties. I have only actually seen four of his paintings, as they are rare and mostly untraceable. I cannot find any records of his having exhibited commercially during his lifetime. However, he did exhibit annually at the Preston Municipal Art Gallery's Local Artists Show. While visiting George Murray, a knowledgeable collector of local self-taught artists in Preston, during the summer of 1976, I saw two Crossleys—one, a scene of a local bowls match and the other an excellent painting of skaters which very much attracted myself and my companion (the American humourist and writer, S. J. Perelman).

RALPH CROSSLEY
Battle for World Leadership.
ca. 1944

There are a few real primitives (and Ralph Crossley is one) who have a kind of intense madness within their paintings, usually a message of a religious or moral flavour, which is portrayed with the fervour of a sermon by a Southern Revivalist preacher.

The World Fight for Civilisation Championship, a painting of a boxing match, is almost an attempt at a cartoon; he gives vent to his feelings as an older man during the Second World War. We see Winston Churchill as a superathlete knocking out a very weedy and absurdly mustachioed Adolf Hitler, to the obvious admiration of the ringside crowd—most of whose faces (with memory and a little artistic imagination) are recognisable as leading figures of the era. The ring itself is colourfully draped with flags of all nations. This painting is now owned by the artist, Martin Leman.

One mysterious painting is intriguingly titled *My Sister, 1948, Her Soul Has a Fortnight's Notice to Find Fresh Tenancy*.

Crossley painted crudely in hard enamels. He had an excellent eye for composition; the subject matter was often vigorous and complicated but becomes much clearer when looking at the back of the picture where he usually pasted an item from the newspaper which had inspired the painting, or, as in the boxing painting, it is a descriptive "who's who" from World War II. Ralph Crossley was a natural, if somewhat freakish artist and like most northerners his messages were always blunt and to the point.

I V

Ted Wilcox

Early in 1967, the artist, Peter Blake, brought a most extraordinary silk embroidery picture of a pin-up girl by Ted Wilcox into our gallery. We were intrigued. Blake explained that about a year previously he had employed a house decorator named Vincent Smith who one morning brought him an embroidery showing Lee Harvey Oswald being assassinated by Jack Ruby. Smith thought that this picture might be of interest to Peter Blake's American wife. Smith had gone on to explain that the previous evening he had walked home from the pub with an acquaintance named Ted Wilcox who happened to live in the same block of council flats in Chiswick, London.

Wilcox had never invited Smith into his flat before and Smith was surprised to find, on entering the small living room, that the walls were completely covered with colourfully embroidered pin-up girls.

Wilcox was soon introduced to the Blakes. Peter recounted: "As we walked into Ted's flat we immediately noticed a life-sized embroidery of Brigitte Bardot taken from a 1957 issue of the British "girlie" magazine *Reveille*, and that by an amazing coincidence I had used this same photograph at the same time to make a similar painting." Blake was one of the originators of British Pop art.

Blake then arranged for Lionel Levy and myself to view Wilcox's work. I remember the tiny room, with Ted, a small, silver-haired, sturdy fellow, seated at the kitchen table littered with empty beer bottles. Every one of the walls was covered with "tits and bums" protruding from "Vargas" girl bikinis. Some of the figures had familiar faces—Marlene

TED WILCOX
Nude.
Silk embroidery,
12″ × 17″,
1955/1965

TED WILCOX
Nude.
Silk embroidery,
14½″ × 10½″,
1955/1965

TED WILCOX
*The Assassination
of Lee Harvey Oswald
by Jack Ruby.*
Silk embroidery,
13″ × 15″, ca. 1964

Dietrich, Betty Grable, Rita Hayworth, Jane Russell and, of course, Brigitte Bardot. They looked like a blown up collection of old *Esquire* calendars or lurid movie posters of the forties. What made the embroideries so fantastic is that they were meticulously executed in very bright, shimmering silks which gave them an extra sensuous quality, while the modulated texture made them almost three-dimensional.

Ted was born locally, in Brentford in 1909, and his main work had been as a night watchman. He became an embroidery artist by accident (literally) when he was injured while serving with the RAF in wartime. Following a spell in the hospital, he was sent to a convalescent home where he and his fellow patients were encouraged to take up some kind of manual therapy. Wilcox chose embroidery and appliqué, a very unusual occupation for a man in those days. To begin with, Wilcox liked embroidery and followed the general trend which was to copy RAF insignia and heraldic subjects, but he soon felt the urge to experiment with something more artistic and so, copied a library book photograph of Anne Hathaway's cottage. However, being more interested in nubile ladies than old cottages, he had a go at embroidering Marlene Dietrich from a movie magazine photograph. "I was very pleased with it and the rest of the lads thought it was terrific—very sexy! So I went on with the girls."

From the mid-forties, his style and subject matter has hardly changed, but his technique has gradually improved and likewise the quality of the tea towels he uses as canvases.

As with the Lee Harvey Oswald picture, Ted Wilcox sometimes introduces items of international drama, perhaps from a news photo. This is quite difficult as he usually traces the outline of the photo on to the cloth and then starts stitching. Each picture will take up to three months to complete. The fully embroidered backgrounds are of an abstract pattern.

As a self taught artist, Wilcox pre-dated the Pop artists, Lichtenstein, Jasper Johns, Peter Blake and others. He discovered that by blowing up a popular image, you can often get something more interesting and exciting than the original.

We decided to hold a one-man exhibition at Portal in May, 1967 and although it was very favourably reviewed (in fact, British art critic Robert Melville bought one for his own collection), the public was not quite ready for them. Sales were slow. We are currently trying to persuade Ted to have another exhibition in the near future. Among the few who did realise the beauty of Wilcox's work was the humourist S. J. Perelman who was so fascinated with this "tea towel" artist that he wrote a short story about him which appeared in the *New Yorker*.

V
Patricia Neville

Patricia Neville will coyly tell you she was born of British parents in Colombo, Ceylon, during the reign of King George V (which ended in 1936). Pat's attractive and youthful appearance certainly suggests that she was born during the latter part of HM's reign, and one would never guess that she is the mother of eight grown children.

As a youngster, she lived mostly in England and studied at the Bartlett School of Architecture. Before she married, she became assistant to the theatrical and film designer, Hein Heckroth. When the last of her children started school, she began to paint again seriously. As she says, "Prior to that time I always dabbled, but I was determined to start in earnest as soon as I had the opportunity." Over the years, Pat gradually became fascinated with the lives of famous British eccentrics and began to thoroughly research the subject. She had been inspired by reading Edith Sitwell's books on the subject. Realising that she herself was not a natural writer, she decided to turn her research into paintings.

The results were delightful and have been very successful. Despite her own modesty about the work, we felt that Pat was ready for an exhibition in 1973. Her completely intuitive technique does justice to her fascinating choice of subjects. She uses very bright colours in her foregrounds and a soft, almost eighteenth century, misty quality for her backgrounds which are as finely detailed as the prominent figures in front. She creates a mystical atmosphere completely in keeping with her eccentric choice of subject matter. For example: such delightful "loonies" as the Countess of

PATRICIA NEVILLE
Grimaldi Collecting Butterflies.
Oil/board, 24″ × 20″

PATRICIA NEVILLE
Eilmer of Malmesbury.
Oil/board, 12″ × 18″

Desmond who, throughout her life, had a penchant for climbing trees and died in 1732 at the reputed and fantastic age of 140 as the result of a fall from an apple tree; Jeremy Hurst who, in the 1840's, rode on a harnessed and saddled bull whilst hunting around Doncaster, accompanied by his sagacious pigs which he used as hounds; Eilmer of Malmesbury, of whom William of Malmesbury, the 13th Century chronicler, relates, "Eilmer, skilled in mathematics and astrology, fixed wings to his hands and feet, ascended a lofty tower and was born upon the air for the space of a furlong. However, owing to the violence of the wind, Eilmer fell to the ground and broke both his legs, claiming the cause of his failure 'as that he forgot to afix a tail on his backside.'" There is Balwin Le Petteur who held 110 acres of land in the county of Suffolk and "before the sovereign Lord the King, shall perform altogether and at once, a leap, a puff and a fart (*unum soltum, unum siffletum et unum bumbulum*)!"

Without doubt, Pat Neville's most exciting discovery during her research was confirmation that she is a descendant of Harry Winstanley, whom she had painted in her first exhibition. Winstanley was born in 1644 at Saffron Walden, Essex, and became clerk of works to King Charles II and of his property at Newmarket. Among Winstanley's achievements was the design and construction of the first Eddystone Lighthouse. He was captured from the lighthouse by French privateers and taken to France, but Louis XIV released him, saying he was at war with England and not with humanity. Winstanley was returned to Eddystone Rock, where he perished during the great gale of 1702. Her first show was favourably acclaimed by critics and collectors who bought the entire exhibition.

PATRICIA NEVILLE
Squire Mytton.
Oil/board

Pat spends little time at the family home in Wimbledon, as her husband Tony, who travels extensively in his job as an executive for ICL, is required to live abroad for lengthy periods of time. We have received parcels of paintings from as far afield as Egypt and New Zealand (her current temporary home), but it was during an enforced two-year stay in Moscow that Pat became fascinated by the life of the nineteenth century comic genius, Joseph Grimaldi. She found that although there had been thousands of souvenir items sold during his lifetime (in his heyday he was as popular as the Beatles), there had been only two serious books

PATRICIA NEVILLE
Grimaldi and Five Cats.
Oil/board, 20″ × 24″

opposite:
PATRICIA NEVILLE
*Grimaldi in
his Lambeth Garden.*
Oil/board, 24″ × 20″

46

about him since his death in 1837—*The Life of Grimaldi* by Charles Dickens under the pseudonym "Boz" and a recently revised book by Richard Findlater in the 1950's. Excellent as these books are, they could not possibly have been far reaching enough to keep the name of Joseph Grimaldi remembered by the public.

Pat Neville looked further into "Little Joey's" very colourful life and decided to paint a complete exhibition of "Incidents in the Life of Joseph Grimaldi." These thirty paintings took her four years and were exhibited at Portal early in 1978. Publishers Jonathan Cape were so enamoured with the series that they commissioned Pat's eldest son, Giles, to write a text to accompany the paintings. The book was called *Incidents in the Life of Joseph Grimaldi* and was published in 1980.

Joey Grimaldi was the son of the eccentric Italian-born comic dancer and pantomime artist, Guiseppe Grimaldi, and Rebecca Brooker, a Drury Lane dancer. It has been suggested that Grimaldi senior was also the royal dentist (in his spare time, no doubt). We do know for certain that he was an overbearing and intolerant father, a notorious womaniser, suspicious of even his closest friends. He was deeply morbid and where phobias were concerned, he made Edgar Allan Poe look like an amateur!

Charles Dickens tells how Grimaldi senior arranged to be laid out in a coffin, suitably dressed and powdered to test the affection of Joey and his younger brothers when they were confronted with the shock of their dead father. However, the cruel trick misfired when the youngest Grimaldi noticed that his "dead" father's chest was moving and whispered loudly to Joey that he thought dead people did not breathe!

Joey was already appearing on the stage at Sadlers Wells when he was three years old. He was a natural clown and at an early age became as famous off-stage as on, for his eccentric antics. During his lifetime, he became a national character and a friend to many notable figures of the period, including royalty. His range as an actor was extensive—bucolic comedy to dramatic pathos, acrobatics and "abracadabra" magic. The make-up which he wore both on and off stage was based on the *commedia del'arte* and was the prototype of all the great clowns. His influence has been great and extends to Charlie Chaplin, Buster Keaton, Marcel Marceau, Jacques Tati and many others.

Unlike his father, he was a gentle, sweet-natured man, a passionate, sincere lover and collector of butterflies. At one period he had the best collection in England, later stolen from him by burglars.

Joey died in 1837, after several years of ill health, pain and suffering. He was unable to walk for the last few years, due to chronic arthritis, as he had broken many bones during his acting career which were usually improperly set. He never complained however, and thanked God for his wonderful life. Fortunately, he completed his autobiography a year before his death. The manuscript was given to his friend Charles Dickens to edit and publish. The last words of his autobiography were: "In my solitary hours, and in spite of all the kindness of my friends, I have many of them in my thoughts, which often dwell afar in the past, and there is one circumstance which always affords me unmitigated satisfaction; it is simply that I cannot recollect one single instance in which I have intentionally wronged man, woman or child and this gives me great satisfaction and comfort."

He was buried in an East London cemetery where, in 1978, clowns from all over the world gathered at the little chapel adjoining the graveyard, to pay their respects on the 200th anniversary of Joseph Grimaldi's birth. Pat Neville's carefully researched and meticulously executed paintings also pay tribute to this great man.

In the painting, *Signor Grimaldi in his Lambeth Garden*, we see the father seated in a silk tunic, and young Joey without make-up in the front. Old Grimaldi cursed the "Ingleesh climate" and when the garden of his house in London was covered in snow (it was January) and he longed for sunny Italy, he decorated the trees with gaily coloured wax fruits and flowers and insisted to his family and friends that it was really summer.

In another painting, Pat shows Joey with high wire artists in full swing during his heyday. Another painting shows Joey surrounded by a feline audience sitting on the roof of a Thameside theatre, amongst the spring blossoms, playing a tune on his fiddle.

Pat Neville is currently living in New Zealand where she is preparing a future exhibition of more eccentric characters.

V I

Richard Parker

Richard Parker, now in his late twenties, spent his formative years in Southport, a handsome and neglected Victorian coastal resort in North West England.* From an early age he was determined to become an artist, and by 1969 had enrolled as a student in the local art school at Harris College, Preston. His art training continued for almost four years (he attended Winchester Art College from 1970), but as he himself says: "The only reason I stayed at art college was to gain a qualification."

Richard Parker is a paradox, a fully trained artist who then trained himself to paint. After leaving college, Richard disciplined himself to a vigorous purging of the influences that had been inflicted on him by a series of mediocre and apathetic tutors. He began to develop a painting style of his own about which he says: "On leaving art school in 1974 I made my way to Yorkshire where I found many beautiful Tudor, Queen Anne and Georgian shops, particularly in York itself, which I consider to be England's most interesting county town. The superb architectural detail of these buildings made me determined to find a suitable style in which to paint them. Up to that time, the only style I had practised was large, splashy, semi-abstract paintings which gave me very limited satisfaction. I wanted to learn the neat craft of observation and recording.

"I started by doing pencil drawings and watercolours of the places that I was most attracted to in my own village and then progressed to oil

* For other noteworthy "Sandgrounders," see my Introduction.

painting on canvas. Because the buildings were made of bricks, I thought that I must try and build up the house and the patterns of the brickwork by starting from the bottom and painting each small part as if I was building the house myself. It was incredibly difficult and the initial results were coarse, despite all the time I put into them. However, I felt that with

RICHARD PARKER
Broadgate, Ludlow.
Oil/board, 18″ × 20″,
1979

51

enough practise, I would make progress and this now seems to be happening for me.

"By 1978, I felt that it was time to exhibit, and I showed my work to the Portal Gallery after a couple of small exhibitions at home in York." We accepted some of Richard's paintings for our summer "miscellany" and they were much admired. His superfine detail and accuracy are almost photographic, and a gentle flavour of naiveté prevails. He paints what he sees, occasionally using a little artistic license to enhance a composition.

RICHARD PARKER
York Minster.
Oil/board, 24″ × 20″, 1982

In *York Minster from the City Walls*, Parker shows a view of his favourite city, seen from the city walls looking southwest. We see, through his eyes, the glorious "mish-mash" of architecture, stretching through seven centuries. In the foreground are the long gardens. Amidst the foliage are glimpses of the ruined ancient abbey, finely detailed, little Georgian houses with minute walled gardens, the rear of the 17th century Treasurer's House and, above all this, floats the historic and

RICHARD PARKER
The Feathers, Ludlow.
Oil/board, 17″ × 18″, 1979

magnificent York Minster. Another superb, small walled town, which took from 1160 to 1500 to complete, is Ludlow in Shropshire near Wales. It has long been one of my own favourite British towns. In his painting, Parker has managed to encapsulate the atmosphere of the town in the view leading from the river to Broadgate. He even includes the rather incongruous "Walls" ice cream sign which he is too honest to ignore, reminding us we are in the 20th Century.

Returning to his beloved York, Richard paints a scene of the outdoor market behind the Shambles. We see a fine example of his tremendous detail in a series of vignettes which are almost still lives of farm produce and in the background, the famous "Cross of York" fishmonger's stall.

At the moment, Richard Parker is working on a series of paintings of Kew Gardens in London and the splendid Victorian hot houses which are to be found there.

VII

William Towers

William Towers is Preston, Lancashire born and bred. He was born in 1934, to be exact. Although Mr. Towers senior was a painter and decorator, William was in no way influenced by him. Most of the other members of Williams' family were in the local cotton mill industry, the "dark satanic mills" (as described by William Blake).

At the age of 15, William became a grocery assistant. Then he joined the army to do his National Service from which he was honourably discharged with the rank of Corporal after two years. After this spell in the army he returned to his native Preston where he worked as a shoe salesman until 1972, when he was invited to stay in Leicester by a friend. He decided to move to the area and got a job in the local boot and shoe industry. As he says: "There was not much point in my staying on in Preston as both my parents were dead. However, when I moved to Leicester I took thirty or maybe more boxes of fabric scraps which my mother had accumulated throughout her working life in the cotton mill, along with numerous unbleached table cloths in drawers and cupboards.

"I was very sad when my parents died and became a lonely person. I started to read the bible, although not for religious reasons. I liked the stories and I decided to make some pictures. I started with Adam and Eve. I was at that time working at night and as it was very quiet at work I took the pictures with me to make them. I first of all felt that I should paint the bible stories, but I had no paints or any idea how to start, and it seemed natural to take some of my mother's scraps of cotton and colour

WILLIAM TOWERS
Name That Tune.
Fabric collage,
22″ × 17″, 1981

them with household dye. I then cut them into squares and put them in batches in buckets of water to make the colours stronger or weaker by diluting them. I then made stretchers and cut out the various coloured cottons to make a picture.

"George Murray, a Preston art collector I knew, heard about my pictures and introduced me to an American lady. This was in about 1971 and friends of hers wrote to me and I started to sell a few pictures to collectors in Los Angeles. I did not like to sell them, but it was nice to get letters from America and people asking to buy them without even actually seeing them. The pictures are all very personal and I can read them by the different pieces of material I have used so I know just whose pillow case it was I used, and each piece of material is like a souvenir of my childhood and the past. I still have lots of rags left which are for pictures, yet to be made, of a time when I was happy with my parents and brothers and sisters. When I moved to Leicester, I began to work on subjects besides the biblical ones, like childhood memories, dance bands, sports and animals. I always try to make a scene accurate."

In 1973, when William came into the Portal, his work immediately struck us as being that of a genuine primitive, closely akin to that of Elizabeth Allen, another fabric artist. It was during the mid-seventies, when Towers began work on his very bold pictures of local people, events, nostalgia and excellent cats, that he really began to take off as an artist. The biblical subjects had restricted him, although his superb colour sense and composition was in evidence from the beginning. I particularly admire Towers' subtle gradation of muted colours, often restricting him to a very limited palette. He shows excellent taste in placing one fabric or colour next to another.

William Towers' most recent pictures are full of humour (like William himself) and are amongst our gallery favourites. I once asked William how he got the patterned sections of his pictures. "Oh," he said, "I cut up my shirts or old pyjamas. When I buy shirts I always look at them with the possibility of a future picture in mind!"

Since 1979, William Towers has managed to sell enough of his work to survive as an artist, a commendable achievement in a field where many artists have to supplement their income by taking outside jobs.

WILLIAM TOWERS
Well Done, Chaps. Fabric collage, 22″ × 17″, 1981

VIII

A. W. Chesher

During the ten years that I knew A. W. Chesher, he always referred to myself and my partner as Mr. Lister and Mr. Levy, and we in return always called him Mr. Chesher. Even today I am not certain that his Christian names were really Arthur William. He was sixty-seven when I met him, and, like several of our artists, he came from the Arthur Jeffress Gallery. He visited us on the suggestion of Robert Melville, the manager of the Gallery, who closed it after Jeffress' tragic death.

Mr. Chesher was the definitive English countryman, spoke with a soft Bedfordshire accent and always wore heavy tweeds, a cloth cap and sparkling black boots. When you met him, his manner was such that you felt he had never performed a dishonest act in his life.

Mr. Chesher was born in Bedfordshire in 1895 and died in 1972. His heritage was farming and his life was totally bound up with the land. As a boy he worked on his father's farm and like any youngster he became enthralled with those great puffing, fire breathing monsters—the steam traction engines. He tells how thrilled he was to be allowed to drive one at the age of sixteen and how even then he knew every different type of engine. His passion for the engines and every form of steam agricultural machinery remained with him throughout his life.

He married quite young and was a devoted husband, but he and his wife were childless and as the years went by they both found solace in religion. Chesher was forced into premature retirement in his mid-forties when he became disabled as the result of two tragic accidents; a gun

A. W. Chesher
Taskers Little Giant.
Oil/board, 14″ × 18″, 1964

backfired when he was shooting crows one day, causing him to lose an eye, and shortly afterwards he caught his arm in a threshing machine which resulted in almost total disability on one side. Robbed of the opportunity to work on the farm and drive his beloved "monsters," he turned to painting. Here was yet another example of misfortune turning foster parent to a new primitive talent.

Chesher felt he had a specific job to do. His fascination with steam traction engines and an incredible, almost photographically accurate memory, led him to make paintings of the old machines with a detailed fidelity which is unmatched in any museum. He would purposely paint them in all the bright and shining colours they were originally given. From the day he started, until a year or two before his death (when, due to his wife's death he completely lost the impulse to paint), all his pictures were of his beloved "monsters." He was spurred to greater efforts by the fact that, when he began to paint, the machines were fast becoming obsolete. Steam traction enthusiasts were amazed with his total recall. In some twenty-five years, Chesher painted about 300 pictures which made a unique and complete history of British steam agriculture. He seemed to regard these paintings almost as a duty because unlike steam trains, nobody else had bothered to record the "monsters" of this era.

In 1964 I visited Chesher with the now-famous film director, Ken

A. W. CHESHER
Baverstime.
Oil/board, 1963

A. W. CHESHER
The Foden Steam Wagon.
Oil/board, 12″ × 18″, 1969

Russell, who was commissioned by the BBC to make one of his legendary "Monitor" films about Chesher's paintings, and a steam traction engine rally. Delighted though Chesher was, to be playing an important part in this television feature, he was somewhat displeased by the collection of magnificently restored engines displayed in front of the cameras partaking in a race. He felt very strongly about the old machines and pointed out that they were not built for that purpose.

Being unique, Chesher found that he had two different groups of enthusiasts for his work; experts came to see his pictures because of the important, accurate information they could glean from every detail (he really knew his subject and never put a foot wrong), then there were others who loved the paintings for their colourful and nostalgic views of Bedfordshire.

Often Chesher would include himself in the paintings, as a boy or a young man. Sometimes he would include relatives long dead, but if the figures in the painting showed the direct naiveté of their own rural settings, the same could never be said of the machines themselves. His use of brilliant colours, and his treatment of the shining metalwork enhanced his natural compositions. Chesher's paintings are never dull or boring. He regularly painted one scene a month and his avid collectors waited eagerly for them. Garfield Weston, the famous Canadian collector, once bought half of an entire exhibition. Other collectors of his work are the author, Graham Greene, and the actors, Kim Novak and Peter O'Toole. So far, no British museum has realised the significance of Chesher's unique documentary, and all his works are in private collections. He has had five Portal exhibitions, the last, in 1971, sadly titled "A.W. Chesher's Last Exhibition."

I X

John Deakin

Professional photographers seem to have an affinity for self-taught art. Several of the leading British professional photographers—e.g., David Bailey, Terence Donovan and David Hearn—are all collectors of this style of painting. In certain cases, like those of Neil Davenport and the late John Deakin, they have actually made the jump from photographer to painter. John Deakin worked in his own Mayfair studio and carried out several photographic commissions for *Vogue* during the mid-1930's. When Deakin was in his own mid-thirties, he exhibited at the celebrated David Archer Soho bookstore, which was a haunt of many famous writers and poets of the era.

Perhaps because of his friendship with artist Francis Bacon, Deakin decided to take up painting. Accurate details of his life are scarce, as most of his contemporaries who frequented the old French pub in Soho have long since disappeared.

His work as a painter blossomed in the fifties with his glowing flower pictures and portraits of cockney characters like the Pearly King and Queen and the marvellous portrait of Queen Mary (latterly owned by S.J. Perelman), which appeared in mixed exhibitions in London. All his work was rich in "gypsy" colour, and carefully executed. The portraits had something akin to the great anonymous English and American primitive painters of the 18th and 19th centuries. He also specialised in flower paintings. Usually, each bowl would be full of multi-petalled spring flowers. Placed right in the middle of a table with a chequered cloth, these

works are reminiscent of an interior or still life by Vermeer or van Eyck. The flower paintings were usually on board about twelve inches square.

I was introduced to Deakin's work in 1960 by Michael and Sheila van Bloeman, the Canadian couple who owned and lived in the Troubadour, London's most interesting artist's rendezvous, a coffee house in Earl's Court. I lived for a while at the Troubadour and came to like the Deakins very much. Even among the Van Bloeman's large and superb collection of folk art, they stood out dramatically. Mike and Sheila had bought about forty of John Deakin's paintings for just a few pounds at a local furniture auction where they came up amidst the junk.

This was the start of the very tragic last stage of Deakin's life. He was in his late fifties when he was invited to exhibit a one-man show in the

JOHN DEAKIN
Flowers.
Oil/board, 14″ × 18″,
ca. 1956

opposite:
JOHN DEAKIN
Pearly King.
ca. 1954

Cork Street Gallery. The exhibition had hardly opened when the gallery was forced to close down by the authorities and declared bankrupt. Unfortunately, all the stock on the premises, including the entire Deakin exhibition, was sent to the auction rooms, unrecognised for what it was, and sold for a pittance to help pay off the creditors. The sharp-eyed Van Bloemans were the lucky (and quite legitimate) buyers of the Deakins. They knew nothing of the artist, but decorated great areas of wall space at the Troubadour with these delightful paintings.

Around 1965 I borrowed two portraits from Mike and Sheila to put on display in the Portal window. These pictures drew in a lot of visitors, one of whom was entirely unexpected. A shabby, red-faced, angry, middle-aged man lurched into the gallery, obviously "under the influence" somewhat, loudly declaring in a cultured voice that the paintings in the window were his and demanding them back immediately. This was my first encounter with John Deakin. He cooled off and I phoned Mike Van Bloeman, who explained the situation in detail and invited Deakin to dinner that night. John had no alternative but to accept things as they were, and he subsequently became quite a good friend of the Van Bloeman's.

He continued to paint and brought in a few paintings of tattooed sailors to the gallery for us to sell on his behalf. However, his work had passed its peak, as alcoholism had got the better of Deakin. He was in bad financial straits and spent most of the money that was given to him by friends or that he earned on booze in sleazy Soho joints. Having drunk half a bottle of paraffin (by mistake he claimed), he was in the hospital for several months, came out almost destitute and was soon back on the booze. Mercifully, he did not last long. He collapsed and died on the streets of Soho before reaching his seventieth year.

JOHN DEAKIN
Pearly Queen.
ca. 1954

X

James Dixon

James Dixon, another genuine primitive, was born on Tory Island, off the storm-girt coast of Ireland, in 1887. He died on the island some eighty-five years later, after spending nearly all his life in the same place.

Inevitably, art connoisseurs compare James Dixon with Alfred Wallis. The similarity in their simple lifestyles is obvious and they even share a certain affinity in painting styles. As if this similarity is not enough, both of these artists were also "discovered" by other artists. Just as Wallis was "found" by Ben Nicholson and Christopher Wood, so Dixon was discovered by the contemporary artist, Derek Hill. However, unlike Wallis, who at least was made aware of some artistic respect in his old age, Dixon received little recognition during his lifetime.

Around 1960, Derek Hill, who has a cottage on Tory Island, was painting a landscape and had set up his easel close to the village of West End. After Mass, a small crowd of locals gathered round to watch Hill working. Among them was Jimmy Dixon who told Hill that he thought he could do better and Hill recalled hearing that Dixon dabbled in painting. He usually tried painting the flowers which he found in his sister Grace's garden. He was already an old man and wanted something to do, so, using household and marine oil paint and making his own donkey-hair brushes, he had a go at painting. He used thick paper (never canvas) and his subjects were mainly scenes of the island, the Atlantic Ocean and his vivid memories of events which occurred during his lifetime. Each painting was captioned on the front with his own pencilled description.

Often the date was inaccurate and the spelling erratic, but the meaning was always clear.

In July, 1966, James Dixon had a one-man exhibition at Portal. Derek Hill, who wrote the catalogue introduction, says of Dixon's works, "They are all painter's pictures and not merely the picture making which comprises so much of the output in the art world today, whether in abstract art or figurative painting. It is a hard definition to explain, but it is largely concerned with the texture of paint and the brushwork, as well as an unusual vision of the natural phenomena around." Hill goes on to say that, "The scenes Dixon chooses to paint of the island are the very opposite of picturesque, they are often harsh, rough and ready-made, but they are deeply concerned with the life that an islander lives. Muldoons caught in the nets, fishing boats at anchor, the great East End cliffs of Tormore, they have little to offer people who want a pretty picture. The clumsiness may be called childlike or primitive, but it is true and intimately related to the place where the pictures have been painted."

John Berger, the critic, referred to Tory Island as being like "a boat adrift with wreck-survivors, but with no hope of ever reaching the mainland." It is because of a combination of this wild environment and Dixon's almost total lack of communication with the outside world, that his work is so simple and isolated, natural as Tory Island itself and certainly as primitive as one could find anywhere in Europe today. Perhaps

JAMES DIXON
Muldoon.
Oil/paper, 21″ × 30″,
ca. 1968

Tory Island will be abandoned by the end of this century. Dixon's paintings will then be a unique record of one of the last, lonely outposts of Britain.

Since James Dixon's death and because of his retrospective exhibition on the mainland, there has been an upsurge of interest in painting on Tory Island. Now there are some half-dozen local "self-taughts" working in their stone cottages, but none have the power and honesty of Dixon. Dixon repeated themes, like views of his village and paintings of giant fish. Among the paintings I have chosen to reproduce is the quite extraordinary *Sinking of the Titanic*—from Dixon's imagination. It is an almost totally black painting but is as alive as if it were multi-coloured. It makes me feel closer to that terrible night than any movie or illustration I have ever seen. Also amusing is his view of the British airship, the R 100, above the island. He also painted Alcock and Brown's first Atlantic crossing which terminated on the Irish mainland. Events like this were the most exciting in Jimmy Dixon's life.

In a conversation with his friend Derek Hill, Jimmy once said, "I like painting local views and people who live on the island. I don't know why. I started painting three or four years ago, something for an old man to do, I suppose. I have always been busy you know, either fishing or doing a bit of work on the land. Of course you don't get all that much colour here excepting the blues and greys of the sky and the glistening sea. There's nothing romantic about little boats fighting with crashing waves or cruel winds, what all this talk about primitive art is I don't understand. I like painting natural things, nothing. . . ."

X I

Barry and Philip Castle

The Castles are not a duo of rhythmic tap-dancers as their names might suggest, but a husband and wife who paint in adjacent studios and form their own artistic colony.

Barry is a nickname for the *foine* Irish name, Finbar, which Barry wishes to forget! As the Castles have exhibited together for almost all of their painting careers, I have twinned them in this volume.

Barry and Philip have obviously influenced each other's work enormously and in the area of colour, their separate palettes are almost indistinguishable. Both use a meticulous technique of stippling the paint onto the canvas with a very fine brush stroke, a technique initiated by Philip, and they appear to almost vie with one another over the infinite detail in each picture. Their choice of subject matter is also quite close—they rarely choose to paint anything contemporary.

Philip Castle tends to select his subject matter from medieval religious legends of Southern Europe and the Middle East. The architecture is painstakingly depicted brick by brick, with elaborate cornices and bizarre gargoyles carefully depicted on the palaces and churches of the elaborate citadels. The buildings are always painted from interesting angles with differing perspectives, so the viewer has a privileged look onto rooftops, inside windows, and through courtyards. His work is closely related to Near Eastern illuminated manuscripts, with a flavour of mosaic tiling. Each painting tells a detailed story, perhaps featuring some eccentric potentate. In the paintings, the labyrinths of passages and open doorways add to the mysteries within. Figures appear in fine robes. There are barges on the canals of Venice, and magical, exotic Siennese and Florentine fortified cities.

Barry Castle leaves more to the imagination. Her subjects are idiosyncratic, reflecting her Irish background. She is fascinated by early Christian and pagan mythology, though more recently she has painted rather more

BARRY CASTLE
The House Beside Loch Ness.
Oil/board, 12″ × 16″, 1981

BARRY CASTLE
We Are What We Eat.
Oil/board, 18″ × 11″, 1981

opposite:
BARRY CASTLE
Family Tree
Oil/board, 23″ × 19″, 1977/78

modern subject matter, such as *A Suffragette Playing Croquet!* Her earlier paintings were often set against a background of gold leaf, her figures eccentric and ignoring the conventions of any particular age—long forgotten saints with their strange animals, or medieval circus troops, as in the balancing act which depicts an entire circus family topped by white doves. Barry's painting are often quite absurd and, in another age, she might have worked upon escutcheons for the Royal College of Heralds or upon bas reliefs of the Stations of the Cross for well-furnished churches and cathedrals, or perhaps illustrating the works of a necromancer's

PHILIP CASTLE
The Doge's Dog.
Oil/canvas, 26″ × 32″, 1980

opposite:
PHILIP CASTLE
Pallio Horse Race in Sienna.
Oil/canvas, 26″ × 29″, 1981

journal, or maybe an alchemist's almanac (which could make use of her elaborate use of gold). Wherever her paintings originate from, they never lack charm or whimsical humour. As an example, one of her latest, titled *You Are What You Eat*, which will be shown in her forthcoming series, *Irregulars*, is definitive.

Philip Castle was born in the south of England in 1929. He gave up a career as a nuclear physicist to become an artist, a change which he has never regretted. He has successfully exhibited at Portal since 1969 and at the Hammer Gallery in New York.

Barry was Dublin-born (1935). She briefly attended Dublin Art School, but was asked to leave due to lack of facilities. This discouraged her from painting until many years later and it was only after she married Philip and he began painting that her interest was rekindled and she slowly began again. She had her first exhibition with us in 1973.

The Castles can really be titled "self-taught sophisticates." Each of their paintings contains an exceptionally high degree of craftsmanship, entirely compatible with the subjects that they choose to depict.

XII

Bill Maynard

Long before the Pop Art boom, Bill Maynard was attracting people's attention to the naked garishness of the commercial world. He was a man with great sensitivity to the social problems which surrounded him. He communicated his message of protest in the only way he knew, through his watercolours. It took the later generation of Pop artists to get a similar, if not quite as serious, message over to the public. First and foremost, Maynard was an original, entirely self-taught and, if somewhat limited in his technique, he had no limit to his sincerity and enthusiasm.

A bearded, somewhat frail and withdrawn individual, Bill was a nonconformist from an early age. He was gifted with a perception that approached the supernatural and although his intellectual capabilities ensured him a place at New College, Oxford, the prevailing academic atmosphere was unpalatable to him.

His shyness and love of nature dictated his lifestyle as a nomadic gardener. Through this occupation he developed a passion for insects, especially beetles, and built up a magnificent, fully classified collection. Perhaps the happiest event in Maynard's short life was meeting a gentle and understanding lady, somewhat older than himself, whom he married and settled down with in a small house in Newbury, Berkshire. In a tiny room which Mrs. Maynard still preserves as it was in his lifetime, Bill produced a series of remarkable works of art. Many of these operate simultaneously on different levels: the outside world; the deeply religious; the erotic; or the humourous. They were all philosophical statements in which Maynard calls for a complete overhaul of subjects like advertising, ecology, sociology, and sexual attitudes. Although religious, he was not a prude. It can be seen that even within the confines of his style he was a master of variety, both in subject and composition. His incredibly complex, somewhat garish, but very clear pictures created a transformation of the contemporary world, showing accepted 20th century paraphernalia as the monsters he believed they were. Other pictures were almost like highly coloured charts, complete with contemporary text somewhat like the children's board games of "Snakes and Ladders" or "Ludo."

Bill Maynard would sometimes work for 18 hours a day and produced an enormous number of paintings, perhaps 1,000 or more. Many of these were tiny vignettes, almost icons or miniatures, with a dash of Fernand Leger and erotic and/or religious overtones.

Early in 1967, Maynard exhibited at Portal and was the subject of an in-depth interview with Barry Penrose for *Art News and Review*. The title for the exhibition at Maynard's own suggestion was "Billmania." He told Penrose that he started painting at the age of twenty-eight, after a hitherto wasted and jumbled life. At the same time, he became a convert to Catholicism and began to feel some surging interest in his life. He first exhibited his crude paintings outside the National Gallery where they were sneered at, kicked, and even stolen, but he did meet some interesting and strange people like Mr. Wellington Sloane—a self-styled master in the art of life. When the time came to plan Bill's catalogue for the show, he suggested that Wellington Sloane write the foreword, in his own inimitable style. Sloane agreed and wrote: "HELP! HELP! HELP! What's the matter? You want a key to Bill Maynard's paintings like Alice's to get into Wonderland? No key required to get into Bill's tunnel of love, only two eyes—and lots of love. Makes your eyes hurt your brains more. Where does all that light come from? Anywhere? Nowhere? From all directions. No lights, no shadows, only piercing colour, aided by lines both sinuous and childlike—supposedly. The forms become less childlike the longer we look. Somehow they fit themselves into a towering, crushing whole—a whole that sticks together. The tragic, funny thing sticks in the eye too. Its parts, held together by dangerous and delicate tensions, seem ready to snap the whole thing to bits at any moment. Lots of clues in Bill's pictures or perhaps you already know the meaning of life? Then don't look too long or you will be back where you were before you started."

This whimsical description of Maynard's work is almost a primitive

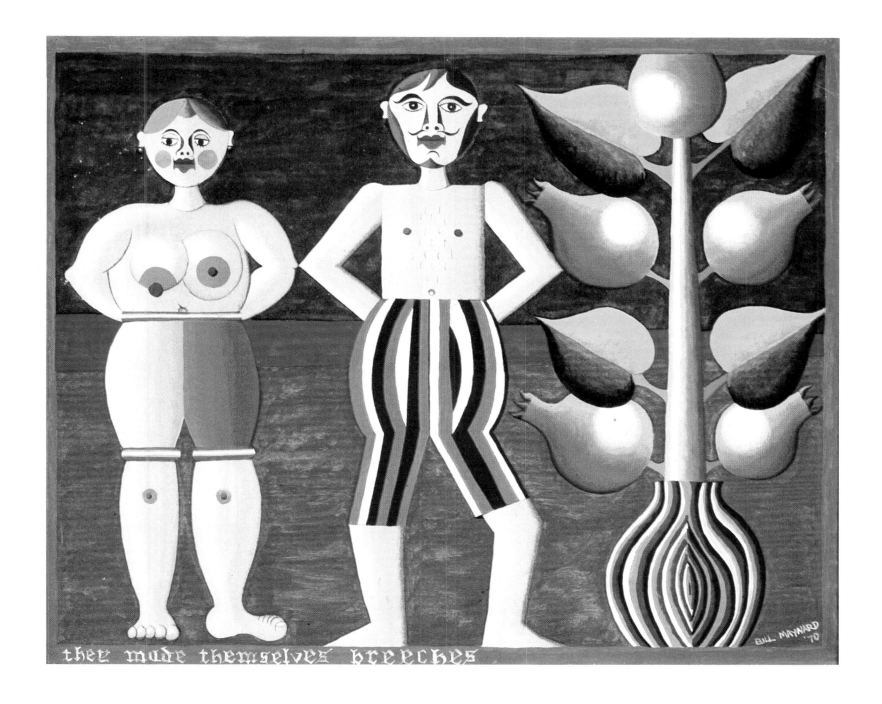

they made themselves breeches

diatribe and, incidentally, was much appreciated by Bill. It seems to be an extension of Bill's own paintings and poetry, which at best is a curious blend of the intellectual, the offbeat, the drop-out and the nutty, but above all is a rare and original talent.

Bill Maynard was on the fringe of a successful career by 1970, with a one-man show at Portal, a retrospective at Hurstbourne Tarrant and a museum exhibition organised by the Brazilian Government where he sold a large number of paintings. His fellow exhibitors were David Hockney,

BILL MAYNARD
Welcome to the Fair.
Gouache/paper,
12″ × 16″, 1966

R. B. Kitaj, Graham Sutherland, William Scott and other famous British artists. His work was selling to collectors on both sides of the Atlantic and we had another one-man show planned for him, when he suddenly became gravely ill and died within a few weeks at his home in Newbury. This was in January of 1971 and Bill was only thirty-seven years old.

He left his life's work and etymological collection to his grieved widow who has to this day kept his studio intact as a shrine.

Lionel, my partner who was particularly keen on Bill's work, recently visited Mrs. Maynard with Barry Penrose who now writes for the *Sunday Times* and they are planning a major article on Maynard's work to coincide with a Portal exhibition in final tribute to this strange, shy man.

XIII

Ralph Bates

Once again the legendary Troubadour appears within these pages. As a home for London's characters and budding celebrities, the "Troubadour University" had a highly successful graduation rate, possibly due to the quality of its "professors." Lenny Bruce, Marcel Marceau, Richard Harris and Bob Dylan were all frequent "lecturers." Even the quality of "dropouts" was superior, and Ralph Bates was a fine example.

Ralph came from Manchester, a Mancunian like myself. He was born in 1931 in the soulless suburb of Moss Side, a perfect example of the Lancashire slums. From an early age he was in and out of countless jobs in restaurants, farms, workhouses, hospitals, forestry, roof tiling and painting fairground novelties. He also did a spell in the British Army on the Rhine.

Somehow, Ralph wound up penniless in the Troubadour during the mid-fifties (it opened in 1954) and Mike and Sheila gave him food and shelter and a part-time washing-up job. He was a prototype of the latter day bearded "weirdo," but he very soon proved that he had a great deal of talent and offbeat wisdom. He produced strange paintings and wood carvings and always carried his painting kit and all his worldly goods with him.

Between 1956–1971 Ralph would suddenly appear and then disappear without warning, sometimes for months and even for years. He travelled by hitching and on foot through Europe, the Middle East, India, Ceylon, Singapore, Indonesia and finally Australia, where he took on labouring jobs to permit him to live in an isolated shack in the bush. Here he painted strange posters carrying his philosophical messages and warn-

RALF BATES
*I Carried Myself
on my Back.*
1955

RALF BATES
The Swing.
Carved and painted wood,
1964

ings to the world (somewhat like Bill Maynard and Ralph Crossley).

Back in London, he joined the Sunday afternoon playgroup in the Troubadour back garden or cellar. Here was the zany Ben Pearl, the Liverpool Jewish playwright who produced and directed his own plays, casting Troubadour habituées in the various parts. A mixture of Alfred Jarry, Ionesco, Damon Runyon and Shakespeare, (if one can imagine such a surrealistic melange), they were, of course, hilarious (even though Pearl was quite serious). Mike van Bloemen asked Ralph Bates to do a series of "one-off" advertising posters for these plays. They turned out to be a series of marvelous primitive graphics, like *I Carried Myself on my Back*—a totally indecipherable play but a superbly dramatic poster—or *I've got Five Pence in my Secret Pocket*. Ralph Bates carved signs and made tiles with medieval troubadours in dark, rich colours. Perhaps his best painted wood sign was for L'Escarpoly, a small French restaurant near Notting Hill Gate.

In 1967, Monique Beau, a French girl of my acquaintance, asked Bates to paint a gigantic mural in the restaurant of a hotel she was designing on the island of Ibiza. Bates found the commission right up his street and agreed with enthusiasm. After all, a paid holiday in Ibiza couldn't be too bad. He made the condition, to which Monique agreed, that he should have complete artistic freedom and privacy whilst working on his mural. He was briefed on what was needed and he agreed. After six weeks' work (during which time he lived in luxury as a guest of the hotel), he unveiled his mural to Monique and the hotel owners, whose immediate dismay was all too obvious. The mural comprised of hundreds of tourists marching in lines from the airplanes onto the island, into the stereotyped hotels which were represented as gigantic and macabre beasts consuming their prey. Needless to say, Ralph was sent back, unpaid, to London. Monique, who kept her appreciation to herself, was reprimanded and the dining room was then covered with flowered wallpaper. Maybe in a hundred years or so, someone will discover the fantastic mural.

Ralph Bates still lives a somewhat nomadic existence. However, he now has a family and works as an itinerant gardener in South London. Very occasionally, he calls into the gallery with a weird painting on board or a watercolour, mostly unsaleable, but decidedly worth collecting. His standard of work is somewhat unpredictable, but his subject matter is always fascinating. Perhaps one day he will settle down to paint an exhibition, but then that wouldn't be Ralph Bates.

X I V

Toby Lyon

People often comment during a Toby Lyon exhibition that he must be
a very observant man. I always reply, "Yes, *she* is." The names Toby Lyon
and Barry Castle may sound like men's, but they are quite definitely not.
Apart from the fact that they are both excellent artists with male names,
they are at opposite sides of the Portal spectrum.

I always consider 1926 to have been an especially good vintage year
for births—slap in the middle of the jazz age, the advent of talkies, the
commonplace arrival of the marvels of the mechanical age, cheap motor-
ing, radio, air travel, absorbing the atmosphere of the depressed thirties,
and then the austere years of World War II. These were part of Toby's
formative years (and mine too), but the few childhood years she spent at
school at Bexhill-on-Sea have remained the most vivid in her memory.

She was born in Birmingham, the daughter of an army officer, and
most of her childhood and teenage years were spent moving up and down
the country. The largest "settled" period was spent in Bexhill. Toby is a
shy, modest, very neat lady who first came to see us in the early seventies.
She invited Lionel and me to go to her studio flat in Earl's Court where
she lived with her husband Peter, a noted sculptor, and her two teenage
children. One, Charlotte, is now a very promising self-taught painter.
Although we appreciated her restrained palette of muted sepias and
creams, reminiscent of Victorian photographs, and her natural sense of
composition, we found her subject matter (pastoral scenes, Swiss landscapes, etc) uninspired. During a pleasant conversation, heavily accented

with nostalgia (people of the same vintage usually remember the same highlights), Toby talked about her memories of Bexhill-on-Sea, a small, almost forgotten Victorian seaside resort in Sussex, and how during a recent visit she had found it virtually unchanged, like stepping back thirty or forty years. I commented that even in the thirties it probably had not changed since Queen Victoria's time, except for a few motor cars and the odd juke box in a seafront cafe. Toby agreed and continued with her humourous observations. Even the local inhabitants and few visitors seemed to her identical to those of her childhood memories. The same painted cast-iron shelters on the Promenade, the old bathing huts no longer in use and the billowing striped canvas deck chairs occupied by one

TOBY LYON
Donkey Rides.
Oil/canvas

opposite:
TOBY LYON
Pink Shelter.
Oil/canvas

90

Toby Lyon, 75.

or two old-aged pensioners and even a donkey man with three forlorn donkeys on the "sands," waiting for the seasonal rush which never actually happened. Summer seemed to have passed by Bexhill. It was grey, chilly and lifeless, but the retired folk wrapped in their unseasonal clothes were ignoring reality and still living in the balmy seaside summers of their younger days.

We all agreed that Toby Lyon should paint an entire exhibition on this subject. By the end of 1975 we mounted *I Do Like To Be Beside the Seaside,* an appropriate title and the name of one of the most famous British Pierrot and holiday concert party songs of the thirties.

Apart from the marvellous compositions of the beach with empty deckchairs and shelters, she painted the little chapels and civic centres, old folks on bicycles, lonely fishermen and even the odd bedraggled sheep on a nearby cliff.

The exhibition was, deservedly a huge success, leading to a second series on the same theme, in 1978. At the moment, Toby Lyon is working on another show of seaside scenes, not all of Bexhill, but some of other seaside havens, which hopefully may remind people to visit them before they are only accessible through albums of faded sepia photographs.

Toby's paintings are not sad; they are saved by the slightly dotty and gentle humour which she manages to find in each situation. Perhaps if she had been born a few decades earlier, she would have been equipped with an ancient wooden box camera, a tripod, black hood and bucket of water instead of oil paints, easel and canvas . . . ?

TOBY LYON
Deckchairs.
Oil/canvas, 12″ × 10″

X V

James Lloyd

I am often asked who is my favourite Portal painter. Even if it is against my momentary commercial judgement, I always reply, "James Lloyd." My criterion is simple. If I were to be banished to a desert island with only one painting, I would select a Lloyd. A kind of "love at first sight" began for me in 1962, when, browsing around the stock room of the late Arthur Jeffress' gallery, I stopped short at a framed gouache leaning against the wall. On closer examination I saw it was painted in a pointillist manner with thousands of tiny dots making each image, but it was obviously a genuine primitive. I was amazed that such an incredible technique could be coupled with such intensely primitive imagery by using gouache on paper and a spectrum of colours which were as fresh as the English countryside. Art critic, Robert Melville, who was in charge of the gallery, agreed with me that James Lloyd was unique and a very special country artist. The picture I was looking at was of children, quite aggressively plain, playing under a rustic, hooped archway of roses. Every detail was made of minute dots which made the composition as a whole strikingly bold and powerful, somehow graphically reminiscent of Ben Shahn. Robert kindly showed me a few more, of sheep almost leaping out of the painting, gigantic farm horses and quite grotesque people. Every tree, every blade of grass, every hair of every animal was executed with meticulous care which must have taken hundreds of working hours, not to mention a rock-steady hand and very sharp eyes, but above all, immense patience and an over-ridingly powerful obsession. Lloyd's style

was the most original I had seen in contemporary painting for many years. Melville told me more about the artist and I grew more excited.

Lloyd was a middle-aged Yorkshire farm worker who had shown with Jeffress a couple of years back and was still painting with gusto. Melville thought that James Lloyd would be glad to hear from me, as he had no London gallery at that time. I wrote to Lloyd and did not have to wait long for a reply.

Late one morning, a tall, ruddy, heavily built man wearing a navy blue suit, scarf and cloth cap came into the gallery, looking like a village "bobby" on his day off. He was carrying a large flat brown paper parcel tied with twine. This he leaned against the wall and then sat down to mop

JAMES LLOYD
Nudes in the Wood.
Gouache/paper,
21″ × 14″, 1968

his brow with a red-spotted handkerchief. Up to now he had not spoken, as he was somewhat out of breath, but he looked and smiled at Lionel and me with his piercing friendly blue eyes. When he spoke, it was in loud, resonant tones with a rich, north country accent. After introducing himself as James Lloyd, he told us that he had walked from Euston Station (about three miles) and was "bloody 'ot" and asked us where he could get a pint of ale. We liked him immediately and when he had very slowly, and with great ceremony, opened his parcel of paintings, we were not disappointed. All his pictures were on soft board and measured about 22" by 14" (a few were smaller). The glowing pointillism was quite incredible. Almost every painting hit you like a fist. His animals—mainly cows and sheep—were reminiscent of ancient cave paintings. The human figures were downright ugly, but utterly fascinating. His subject matter was quite bizarre; backgrounds of tree avenues were painted like sentinels and were all done with meticulous precision. We were moved by the man's obvious sincerity and his northern, forthright manner.

I took him to lunch that day; it comprised several pints of the best bitter (beer) at the local pub. I sipped my half pint and watched him in awe! Needless to say, the pork pie he had ordered and left untouched, was later carefully wrapped in the same brown paper he had brought his paintings in and squashed into his pocket for the train journey home, no doubt to be accompanied by another dozen pints, I thought.

Lloyd outlined his life story, punctuated with a lively sense of humour. He told us that he was born in 1905 (he was now in his late fifties) in Alsager, Cheshire, and that his family were farmers. He was a typical country boy, always keen on drawing and had won second prize in art at the local school when he was thirteen. At seventeen, he managed to sell a black and white study to the local policeman on condition that he made another to match it. The price agreed upon for the pair was £1. After long working hours on the farm, he would go home and paint, trying to copy the great English artists, Constable and Turner, whom he had seen in library books and particularly admired.

During the late twenties and thirties, James Lloyd continued painting, but quit the farm, and worked his way around Lancashire and Cheshire doing a variety of jobs. He was at times a builder's labourer, a lamp lighter, a gas works stoker, and a bus conductor. He even became a policeman for a short period. This last occupation obviously helped him be accepted for the famous and exclusive British Army regiment of the

JAMES LLOYD
Self-Portrait as Rousseau with Violin.
Gouache/paper
20" × 14", 1966

Coldstream Guards. There is a marvellous painting by James of a guards-man in full dress uniform marching down a country lane. He served with distinction in his regiment overseas during the war, though he was older than most of his fellow soldiers. On demobilisation, he married Nancy; she was a teenager and he was in his forties. He returned to the land and took a job as a waggoner in Shropshire.

James was now settled with Nancy and over the years they had nine children, eight of whom survived. Apart from his fatherly duties he felt a great desire to paint again. The family moved to Yorkshire in 1950, to a small village called Skirpenbeck, outside York where, in 1953, he took a job as a cowman, devoting all his spare time (except for the pub) to his painting. He worked out his style of painting with a strange individual shrewdness. By looking intensely at reproductions and photos in weekly

JAMES LLOYD
Tree.
Gouache/paper,
14" × 21", 1968

98

farming journals, he saw that the reproductions (in those days letterpress, offset litho was yet to come) were printed from a series of screens, using one for each colour, and with a magnifying glass he could see how all these illustrations both in colour and in black and white were composed of hundreds of thousands of minute dots. With immense patience, he worked out how to copy this photographic technique and he began to copy pictures from local newspapers. He used old paint brushes discarded by children, because most of the hairs had fallen out, and a Woolworth's children's water colour set. To save money, he even made his own Christmas cards for a few years. Unfortunately, very few of these seem to have survived.

JAMES LLOYD
Cat and Mouse.
Gouache/paper,
14″ × 21″, ca. 1966

When Jim was painting away at the kitchen table at night, he would be oblivious to the cacophony of the family and the television. Nancy was his severest critic and, in 1956, she decided it was time that Jim's work was seen by more people. The problem was how; he had only sold a few paintings locally for paltry sums, and they did not know anyone in the art world. Without telling Jim, she went to York and found the Austen Hayes Gallery. She also visited the City Art Gallery where she was advised to write to John Jacob, the curator. She also found out that the celebrated art critic and historian, Sir Herbert Read, lived in the area.

Within a few days, Austen Hayes had accepted some of Jim's work. He liked it but wondered if it was too primitive for the conservative population of York. Sir Herbert, with fellow art critic John Berger, in

JAMES LLOYD
Sheep.
Gouache/paper,
14″ × 21″, ca. 1964

JAMES LLOYD
Lifeguard.
Gouache/paper,
7″ × 10″, ca. 1959

response to an invitation from Mrs. Lloyd, arrived at the little house to meet James and look at his work. They were obviously very impressed and after spending some hours in his company paid him £100 for several paintings. James couldn't remember how many, as he was so excited to make the sale! At the same time, John Jacobs, curator of York Museum, visited the Lloyds and was deeply impressed, although he did not quite know where to "place" it. It was not until 1957 that anything really significant happened about James Lloyd's work.

John Jacobs had moved to Liverpool and met critic Robert Melville, who was an associate of the Arthur Jeffress Gallery. Melville was in Liverpool to review John Moores' exhibition at the prestigious City Walker Art Gallery. He told Melville all about Lloyd. This resulted in Lloyd's first one-man show in London, at the Arthur Jeffress Gallery in 1958. Jim and all the family were immensely proud, and all but two of the thirty-two paintings were sold. Jim was puzzled that "posh" people were really interested in his paintings. Shortly after this, the rapidly expanding Lloyd family moved to a council house in the village and Jim took a job with the Derwent Plastics Company at nearby Stamford bridge—the money was better and the hours easier. So, with the impetus and the financial help of a successful exhibition, he put even more time and obsessive spirit into his work. He began painting all manner of different subjects, e.g., celebrities of the period. To amuse his children, he copied popular singers and film stars from the newly acquired television which he played constantly while painting. He made pictures of country scenes— no one painted animals with such close observation. James Lloyd was quite prolific; he painted fifteen to twenty paintings a year, from the most bizarre to very sweet subjects, some tender and even some erotic pictures, like the small painting of a lifeguard wading through the water to the beach, carrying the lifeless body of a young girl bather, a deeply touching picture of an incident that had taken place at a nearby seaside town and he had read about in the local newspaper.

He painted an odd copy of the famous Duccio painting of *St. George and the Dragon*, a strange, compelling painting of his family and their pets, a still-life of apples lying in the grass, and an amusing, very sensuous painting of naked girls cavorting in a forest. Jim said about this painting: "It were them hippy tarts," he had seen in the woods.

Gradually Lloyd's fame spread. Amongst his earliest patrons were the noted collectors, Lady Christine West and Mr. Tom Laughton (brother to the actor Charles Laughton), who both built up fine Lloyd collections. Laughton owns a painting by Lloyd of the preacher, John Wesley, which was painted on the back of an old washstand mirror in oil paints, (a media he used extremely rarely).

In 1961, Jim was commissioned by the York City Art Gallery under the Evelyn Award Scheme to paint a view of Clifford's Tower in an ancient part of the city. This was Jim's first painting to be in a public collection and naturally he was delighted.

Shortly after Jim joined us in the early sixties, I introduced him to the then up-and-coming film maker, Ken Russell. Lloyd was just the type of character that Russell liked and the result of their meeting was a BBC film for the programme *Monitor* entitled *The Dotty World of James Lloyd*. It was an excellent production which showed Lloyd's paintings to full advantage and his simple, family life, all filmed on location in and around his home. Russell's film became a classic and is still played by the BBC from time to time. The effect of the film on Jim's life and on the success of the Portal Gallery was almost immediate. In 1964 there were only two TV stations in Britain and luckily for us, channel One went on strike on the stormy Sunday evening that Russell's film was shown, timed to coincide with our exhibition of Lloyd's work which was to open the next day. As a result, it was watched by about fifteen million people. As I sauntered along Bond Street at about ten the next morning, I noticed what looked like a crowd outside the gallery—these were in pre-parking meter days and a long line of cars was parked outside. Until I reached the door with the keys in my hand I had no idea that these people were all waiting for the Lloyd exhibition to open. It was like an avalanche! Some fifty people tried to squeeze into the tiny gallery, everyone was talking loudly and at once, and the phone was ringing continually. As Lionel was in Liverpool, I called a girl friend, and by chance the American artist Tibby Levy came by, so with the help of these two ladies, the entire exhibition of thirty-five paintings was sold in only two hours. The portrait, now owned by Mr. and Mrs. Ken Russell, of the newly-famous Beatles, was the center of attraction in the window, together with a superb sheep painting which was bought by the actor John Mills. The gallery was like an auction house; no sooner was a painting sold than another client offered the buyer a profit on it. This enthusiasm continued for the entire month the show ran. We ensured James Lloyd that he could give up his factory job to become a professional artist. He came down to London during the

JAMES LLOYD
Boy and Horse.
Gouache/paper,
21″ × 14″, 1965

exhibition and was obviously hugely flattered to be so praised by all these "posh" people. Of course, he remained quite unchanged, especially in his love of beer and his gambling on the horses, but, although he was now better off financially, he only put an extra shilling or two on a horse and just treated more people in the pub. We always arranged for him to stay in a modest, convenient hotel in Notting Hill Gate when he came down to London. He soon became a very well-liked character, usually to be found in the bar till the small hours!

He used to come to the gallery three or four times a year and really enjoyed his trips to London. He insisted on being paid weekly, in the form of a regular wage, so he could collect it every week from his local bank. This gave him the security he and his family needed, but apart from a few items like a washing machine and a new "telly," most of his increased income went to provide for his children.

The sixties were exhilarating for James Lloyd. Following the success of the TV film, Russell approached him again and suggested that Jim play the part of Douanier Rousseau in the film on the great French, naive artist he was about to make for *Monitor*. Jim was very surprised when Russell asked him to do the part. It was Russell's inspired idea that the two men, although from totally different backgrounds, would readily identify with each other. Lloyd was persuaded to take the part, and, with a minimum of coaching from Russell, who allowed Lloyd to improvise his spare lines, the film was superb. Jim and the other players were entirely natural, and the flavour of Rousseau's naiveté came over with total sincerity.

Before this film, Jim knew little about Rousseau, but after playing the part and reading about him, Jim said how well he understood the frustrations and happy moments of this great artist's life. As a kind of tribute and souvenir of the film, Jim painted three self-portraits as Rousseau. One of the best is of him as Rousseau, out in the fields, playing a fiddle.

Lloyd was very favourably reviewed by the British critics, who rarely pay much attention to self-taught artists, and he was acclaimed in the *Observer*, the *Sunday Times*, the *Telegraph*, the *Daily Express*, the *Evening Standard*, the *New Statesman*, the *Yorkshire Post*, the *Spectator*, the *Guardian*, the *Daily Mirror*, the *Eastern Daily Press*, and the *New York Herald Tribune*. His brilliant painting *Cat and Mouse* was acquired by the Tate Gallery, an honour of which he was justly proud. He also corresponded with the famous British artist, L. S. Lowry, who had admired his work, and they eventually swapped a couple of paintings. Lowry wrote the foreword to Lloyd's 1971 exhibition. Other galleries who acquired his work were Leeds City Art Gallery, York Art Gallery, the Bowes Museum, and St. Thomas' College, York. He was also noticed by collectors abroad and his work was brought by museums as far apart as Carracas, Venezuela and Zagreb, Yugoslavia. In Zagreb, he won the coveted International Best Primitive painter award in 1973, with his painting *Boy with Horse* (1965), an immensely powerful painting that was praised by the well-known and insular, French, art critic, Anataole Jakovsky, in his book *Peintres Naifs* (1967).

James was unaffected by his acclaim, but he very much enjoyed the social side of it. When the Duke and Duchess of Bedford, who have a very fine collection of self-taught artists at Woburn Abbey, invited him, Nancy, and myself to lunch, Jim was bubbling over with excitement. We could not persuade Nancy to get out of the taxi as she was so shy, but that didn't deter Jim from eating a hearty lunch while Nancy sat in the taxi. Eventually, the Duchess and I managed to coax her out and she was made to feel quite at ease by the Duke and Duchess.

The photographer, David Bailey, bought several paintings by Lloyd and became a good friend. When his book *Goodbye Baby and Amen*, an album of Bailey's portraits of celebrities of the sixties, was published, James Lloyd featured prominently. This resulted in Lloyd being invited to a celebration party for David Bailey at *Vogue* magazine. Jim arrived in London about noon and, after a little chat, asked me if I hadn't noticed his new suit. I certainly had, but declined to mention it. It looked like a 1946 demob suit, given to ex-servicemen on leaving the forces. Jim told me he had ordered the suit by mail and it was a real bargain. The fact that the pants were some three inches too long and the jacket sleeves some three inches too short, hardly seemed to bother him, but on my pointing this out he agreed that a fast alteration job might help. I called a client, a Lloyd admirer who happened to be one of Saville Row's most expensive tailors. When I mentioned Lloyd's name, he told me to send him over, and within two hours he had remodelled the suit. When Jim offered to pay, he was told that the pleasure of meeting him had been enough. Now, with Jim looking somewhat smarter, we went over to the *Vogue* party. It was a mass of celebrities and beautiful models. Jim was delighted when people recognised him and paid him compliments, especially beautiful young ladies who seemed to adore his warm, sturdy, old-country charm.

During this reception, the booze was flowing like water and Jim was liberally helping himself to anything that happened to get within two feet of him. He became decidedly merry and, when I pointed out his train would be leaving for York very shortly and Nancy would be there to meet him, he was most reluctant to leave. I finally bundled him into a crowded elevator where he belched and declared loudly, "I'm as pissed as a fart!" Heaving him into a taxi, I decided to accompany him to the station, and when he arrived, he was fast asleep so I decided to put him into a nearby hotel and get him on a morning train. With a lot of good-humoured protests, I finally got him into bed and removed his size ten policeman's boots and his jacket, and, placing a blanket over him, I left

JAMES LLOYD
Boy with Boxer.
Gouache/paper,
14″ × 21″, 1963

108

him snoring soundly. I arranged with the hotel clerk to wake him at 8.00 A.M. with breakfast and make sure he caught the 9.30 A.M. train. I paid the bill, leaving a sizeable tip, and called Nancy to inform her of the change of plan. The following afternoon, Jim came plodding into the gallery, grinning broadly. Naturally, I was surprised. He looked triumphant and said: "You thought I was asleep. Well, I wasn't. I got up and went over to the station hotel for a couple of pints, met some nice people who invited me into the back room for a few more and got back to the hotel about 4.00 A.M.!" "But," I protested, "I asked the porter to wake you up at eight." "Oh, he did," James replied, "I gave him a quid and told him to bugger off." My fears were well-grounded. The cash we had advanced him was all gone in the betting shop and the bar, and he needed some more to get home. He had also forgotten to notify Nancy. I called and said that Jim hadn't felt very well. She knew exactly what that meant, but forgave him on his return to York later that evening.

Lloyd's work reached its peak towards the end of the sixties, when he painted portraits of such diverse personalities as Churchill, whom he depicted sitting at an easel, dressed in characteristic clothes in Morocco, with his back to the viewer. He also painted Nasser, Chuck Berry, and the famous British model, Jean Shrimpton. There is a very moving painting of the village vicar entering his little church, walking away from the viewer. He painted exotic animals, fish, and birds too—dolphins to amuse his children, monkeys, glistening, black crows, and, of course, his marvellous farm animals. James also had his own brand of quite fantastic and amusing eroticism. He painted the dream he had of a tall, naked blond walking through an avenue of trees. Between two trunks appears a horse's head with his mouth open suckling at the lady's right breast. This weird originality was part of a natural and fresh approach to everything he painted.

During 1971, Jim's health began to deteriorate. He had always suffered from bronchial attacks and his recent lack of exercise and fresh air was affecting him. On doctor's orders, he gave up smoking and drinking; this must have been a great blow to him.

He carried on painting as obsessively as ever, but eventually collapsed. After a few days in the hospital, he was sent home, far from well, and I managed to persuade him to visit a health clinic in Scotland. He sent us a painting from the clinic of a plate of salad and told us in a letter that he loved the people but hated the salads. Maybe the painting helped him to show his contempt for what he regarded as "bloody rabbit food."

Despite Nancy's valiant efforts and our persuasion, he would not, and could not, understand how sick he was. He would secretly stuff himself with forbidden foods and, due to a gouty foot, could not take any exercise. He continued painting, even in the hospital, and gave drawings to the nurses, as he could use only a pencil when lying in bed.

He finally died from a multitude of ailments, combined with a heart attack, on March 10, 1974, aged 69. He was buried with a simple ceremony at the little local church in Skirpenbeck.

An obituary appeared in the London *Times*, but perhaps the best obituary was written by his original mentor, John Jacob, who wrote the catalogue for the 1977 James Lloyd retrospective exhibition at the Camden Arts Centre, London (a second retrospective was held at York University in 1979). James Lloyd was an artist with an individual sincerity, directness of approach and care in execution. His work was the result of a perceptive observation of everyday life, particularly in the country things that appealed to him, which he revealed with his own, almost surrealist, vision. He has been ranked with the best of the modern naive painters, but I believe that this exhibition will also demonstrate his kinship with that peculiarly English and American tradition of rural primitive painting which has flourished since the eighteenth century and which, in his loveable way, he showed was still alive!

X V I

Scottie Wilson

Scottie Wilson's origins are almost as enigmatic as his paintings, although the reference books report that he was born in Glasgow, Scotland, in 1890, and he died in London in 1974.

Scottie was something of a romancer and would sometimes deny his Scottish origins. Despite a magnificent Glaswegian brogue, he claimed that his family were Polish Jewish peasants who, when they gained their liberty from Poland, landed at Hull in the north of England and adopted the appropriate name of Freeman. This is a characteristic Scottie tale, but I have a feeling it is not perhaps without some foundation and that he adopted the name Wilson as a young man.

Although Scottie Wilson was too young to fight in the Boer War there is no doubt that he was in the British Army in the years before the First World War. After seeing military service in the East Indies, he claimed to have bought himself out of the army in Bloemfontein in South Africa just before the First World War and then joined the Merchant Navy and travelled the world as a sailor.

It is believed that he left home an uneducated child. Scottie remembered his father, who was a taxidermist, and perhaps in his later paintings of stuffed fish and what appear to be frozen birds, there is a direct influence of childhood memories of his father's work.

Somehow, Scottie arrived in Canada and spent a long period of his life there between the wars, working as a lumberjack in remote areas. Here he became familiar with the North American Indians who interested him

greatly. He befriended them and learned something of their language, customs, and folk lore. Somewhere along the line, he began to paint and, although he was illiterate (he even had friends sign his name on a canvas until he learned to copy it) his watercolours became a kind of calligraphy.

His pictures fall into two categories. The early ones are usually considered his best, and were painstakingly drawn in Indian ink and tinted in cool tones with watercolour. Later, like most primitives, he would use the closest available materials, often thick, opaque gouache on dark paper. The imagery which he selected came from a limited range of subjects and did not vary greatly. Though the French art critic, Anatole Jakovsky, considers his work to be stereotypical, I cannot agree with this.

SCOTTIE WILSON
Untitled.
Coloured inks,
crayon on board,
20″ × 18″

Like a good chef he constantly repeated his best dishes which continued to please. His subject matter was drawn from a world of legends and fables and is entirely timeless. Often fish predominate. Swans, exotic bird and plant life, masks and strange magical faces or butterflies, odd-shaped cones or tower-like structures, large, lush flowers and nearly always dense linear decorations of ghostly forms are all very carefully worked out in a methodical fashion. His world was an amalgam of sweet dreams and nightmares, his visionary mind frozen in time.

During the 1930's, Scottie's work appeared on the art scene and was appreciated by several of Europe's leading authorities. Later, he was selected for Jean Dubuffet's collection *L'Art Brut*. His first London exhibition was at the Gimpel Fils Gallery in 1947 and he exhibited regularly after this in leading galleries in Paris, Belgium and Basel. Scottie appeared in London spasmodically during the fifties and sixties and several prominent British collectors and dealers made sizeable collections of his paintings. Being an artist who repeated themes, he was prolific, and would call into any Mayfair gallery he happened to be passing (he was often broke) and would usually offer his work for the price of a bottle of whisky. Luckily he was made aware of the value of his work by the London collector and dealer, Victor Musgrave, who became a good friend and mentor to Scottie Wilson, and in later years promoted his work in serious galleries. Scottie was also helped in his career by a familiar figure on the Bond Street gallery circuit, the barber and art connoisseur, Andrew Demaine. He would visit us regularly and show us photographs of his specially commissioned "Scottie."

At one time, Scottie would promote his own work, like a showman featuring himself as the sideshow. He actually hired a tent at a seaside resort, hung his paintings inside and placed a notice on the tent flap reading, "Famous artist, Scottie Wilson, Admission 3 Pence." Just after the Second World War, people queued to see Goering's huge Mercedes-Benz staff car, which was on show at a premises on London's Oxford Street. They also found at the same time, an exhibition of Scottie's work on show in the empty shop next door—admission 6 pence!

Scottie's personality matched his individuality of artistic style. As, and when he could afford it, he lived on a diet of whisky, kippered herrings and cheap English "Woodbine" cigarettes. When he was in the money he actually had his cloth caps and boots custom made in Saville Row. Most of the time, however, he lived on his wits and the erratic income his paintings provided, which didn't allow for many such luxuries.

He was always cheery; and his broad Glaswegian accent was a familiar sound in the Mayfair galleries, where he would call in for a chat or to drink himself out onto the sidewalk at a private view.

Sometime during the mid-sixties, he was approached by Royal Doulton to paint designs on a line of table-wear. They paid well and Scottie's plates became quite well-known during his latter years and have often been exhibited alongside his paintings in retrospective exhibitions. He lived mostly in Kilburn, London, and died, aged 84, in 1974.

XVII

John Allin

"What they've done to the East End is diabolical, diabolical. They've just built and built and tore down and tore out and took its identity away and just made it into a concrete nothing..." Possibly somewhat exaggerated, this was, however, spoken with passion, anger and sincerity by John Allin. It appears on the cover of his book (with playwright Arnold Wesker) *Say Goodbye*.

John Allin was introduced to us in 1969 by a freelance TV producer, Rex Bloomstein who had met John in a pub in the East End of London. Bloomstein became interested in this fair-haired, stockily built, very articulate cockney. What particularly fascinated Bloomstein were Allin's views about art and his vivid descriptions of his own paintings. So he visited John's home and, as soon as he saw the work, he realised that John Allin had great talent. His paintings presented, using authentic "street" colors, a complete documentary of the decline and fall of the East End of London, one of the most colourful working class areas, over the past forty years. Rex knew of the Portal and suggested he and John "go up west" to show us his work. We were just as enthusiastic as Rex had been and without delay planned an exhibition. This was in 1969 and we asked John to prepare a short autobiography for the show:

He was born in 1934 in Hackney, very close to where he now lives with his wife and daughter. He was brought up like all East End kids, to be as tough as the next boy. During the bleakest years of the war, the blitz and rationing, he was evacuated with large numbers of his school mates, cockney and Jewish, to what must have appeared to them a foreign country—Wisbech, in the heart of the English "Fen" country. John clearly remembers the day when he and thousands of kids and their mothers, all clasping gas masks and packets of sandwiches, streamed out of Liverpool Street Station to an unknown destination for an unknown period of time.

opposite:
JOHN ALLIN
Joe's Cafe.
Oil/canvas, 20″ × 21″, 1981

above:
JOHN ALLIN
Bakery.
Oil/canvas, 1974

117

Back on the streets of Hackney towards the end of the war, he played and made home-made carts from broken bikes. He sneaked into Saturday cinemas and "nicked" apples from the costermongers' barrows. He jeered at the Salvation Army, chased the girls and picked up a few words of Yiddish. In 1974, he and Arnold Wesker, who had lived on the opposite side of the street and was almost the same age as John, put down the nostalgic story of their early days in a book of paintings and prose called *Say Goodbye* (published by Jonathan Cape).

John joined the Merchant Navy and sailed around the world twice before he was twenty. He served with the Army in North Africa and later held a variety of jobs as a waterboard employee, a tree planter for London parks, a taxi driver and latterly a long distance truck driver, where he earned the nickname "Allin Road," the signature on his early paintings. In the mid-sixties, whilst working in these various jobs, he caught the painting bug. Like other would-be artists he started with a cheap set of oils and tried to copy a Rembrandt; with no previous experience in this medium, the result was a mess. At this time something happened which was to have a profound effect on John's lifestyle. Some stolen goods were found on his truck, he was arrested on a minor felony charge and he was sentenced to six months in an open prison. Part of the "corrective therapy" chosen by Allin was a weekly art lesson where he began to learn the basics of oil painting. His short stay at "Her Majesty's leisure" became the turning point in his life. Up to this time he had been a manual worker. Now he was determined to become a good artist and earn a living as a painter. After copying all the reproductions of old masters that he could find in prison library books and becoming despondent with the rather miserable results, he decided to try and paint what he knew best—the East End. When John was released after a few months, he set to work with great enthusiasm on his new career as an artist, soon discovering that to paint is one thing but to earn a living by painting is quite another. So, to supplement a virtually non-existent income, he worked at part time jobs, and helped out at his wife's family's eel and pie shop, one of the few original cafes which served favourite cockney cheap "nosh"—fish and chip, bangers (sausages) and mash, or eel and mash and pies. These are all still great favourites with the working population of the area.

John devoted all the time he could spare, to painting the old streets, shops, cinemas, markets, synagogues and old Jewish rendezvous, barber shops, baths, men on building sites, and kids playing the games he

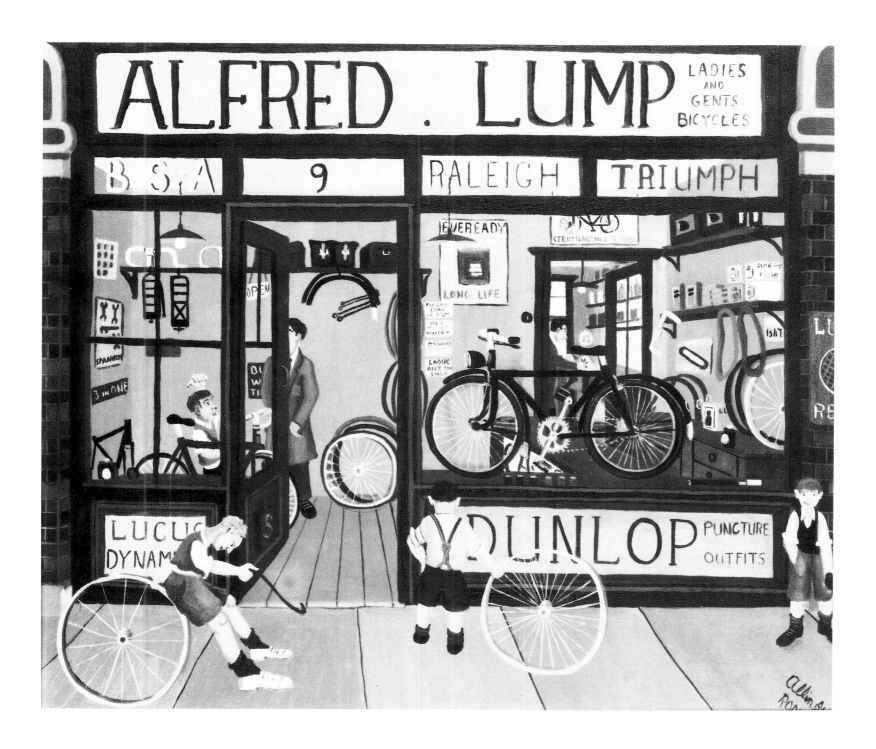

JOHN ALLIN
Alfred Lump's Bicycle Shop.
Oil/canvas, 15″ × 17″

remembered from his own childhood. He painted Wentworth Street, Fashion Street and Petticoat Lane (the world-famous Sunday market) and Gardener's Corner, scene of the notorious battles between Oswald Mosley's British Union of Fascists Black Shirts and the Jews and dockers of the East End. Often John or his family appear in his paintings.

It was these documentary paintings that John brought into the gallery. He explained with gusto that the names over the shops were entirely

accurate. Some of the tiny Jewish dress shops were the beginnings of what are now nationally famous chain stores. Already, his technique was refined and the paintings fresh. So, after appearing in a mixed show early in 1969, he prepared a series of his East End scenes for a joint exhibition with Neil Davenport entitled, *Toffee-Nosed Toffs and Tattered Totters*, meaning that the "nose in the air," snobs painted by the elegant Mr. Davenport, contrasted with the tattered street traders painted by John Allin. John and Neil, though complete opposites became, and still are firm friends.

John's work was well-received by the media who appreciated its directness and honesty. During the early seventies he was the subject of several TV programmes, perhaps the best being a film for *Aquarius* (Thames Television), directed by Humphrey Burton. There was also *Say Goodbye*, written with Arnold Wesker. This magnificent joint effort, now out of print and a collector's item, became the classic book on cockney life in the East End. Allin produced a portfolio of limited edition reproductions and we had a major exhibition to coincide with the publication of the book. The paintings were all sold, and several were bought by people who had never bought an original work of art before, but were now successful business people with East End backgrounds. Among our clients were even some of the little clothing shop owners and proprietors of kosher restaurants which are now well-known names.

John's work was very favourably reviewed and he looked set for success. Perhaps, however, because of his new-found recognition, John was somewhat premature with his future plans and decided upon a complete change of subject matter. He wanted to do a series of paintings and a book, on circus life and consequently joined a small travelling troupe, Gerry Cottle's Circus. He wanted to paint the circus as it had never been painted before—from behind the scenes. He bought himself a motorised caravan to be able to travel with the troupe. They taught John to be a clown, a tightrope walker, and "muck in" with the dozens of odd

JOHN ALLIN
Hackney Baths.
Oil/canvas, 1974

jobs needed to keep the show running. He kept painting everything he saw and stayed with them for almost three years. This turned out to be a mistake. Although the paintings are good, his real forte is still the East End. He was away from the gallery for so long that the demand for his pictures began to dwindle, as we had no paintings to show the impatient clients. Finally, John quit the circus and slowly completed the book which has turned out very well and is to be published by Michael Joseph in 1982.

Once again, John had to take on various jobs to supplement his

income, but he was home and painting his "patch" again. In 1979, John was invited to enter one of his East End paintings, a marvellous scene of a factory, in the prestigious, international exhibition of naive painting held at Morges, Switzerland. The painting won first prize despite the traditional handicap of a rather insular bias on the part of the French and Swiss judges. John was rightly proud to be the first British painter to win this award.

From time to time, John visits us with a newspaper parcel which, when opened, reveals another splendid East End scene like one of his most recent, *Alfred Lump's Bicycle Shop*. We see himself and the other kids begging for Mr. Lump to give them a few used bits so they could build a bike from an old frame they had just found. John is now back on "form" and busy painting for his next Portal show.

JOHN ALLIN
Cockerton and Son's.
Oil/canvas, 22″ × 27″, 1971

XVIII

Fergus Hall

Occasionally a lone figure in literature appears, with an idiosyncratic vision which enraptures the public. This person is outside the mainstream and has a strange quality which almost hovers on the brink of madness, but never degenerates to that level. The work is a fascinating combination of the absurd, the humourous, the phantasmagorical and the world of dreams. Lewis Carroll created such a masterpiece with *Alice*. Edward Lear is another example; his "nonsense" seemed to make more sense than reality. Latterly, the insane anarchistic humour of the "Monty Python" team. The one painter with all these qualities who comes to mind, is Fergus Hall.

Fergus was introduced to Portal by a fellow Scots painter, Patrick Byrne, in 1971. I was immediately captivated by Hall's unique style, and Lionel agreed we should mount a one-man exhibition as soon as possible.

Like some of our other self-taught artists, Fergus had received some formal art training in Glasgow, but rejected it to develop his own, very personal vision. He was brought up in a theatrical environment; his father was a scene painter. Young "Feegie" became attracted to music and painting and taught himself to play the guitar and the mandolin. He would use these instruments to accompany his own poetry. His fascination with the bizarre and curious triggered his desire to become an artist and depict his ideas in paint.

He blends a unique mixture of science fiction and earthy fantasy. No matter how grotesque the figures are that appear in his paintings, they always have a delicious quality of humour which makes them so attractive and never offends. The people, both male and female, with huge shoulders

FERGUS HALL
The Fat Musician.
Oil/board, 17″ × 17″, 1977

and tiny feet and hands, always look benign, never aggresive. The six-legged horses and the curious dogs and cats are obviously friendly creatures.

Fergus Hall's first exhibition was in 1972. The subjects were witches, necromancers, alchemists and angels and some of the poetic titles of Fergus' paintings are worth recording: *Tattoed Lady on Swing with Sunangel, Lola Kissing the Black Angel, Magus In his Flying Machine, The Astronomer Who Stole the Stars.* Fergus' work varied in size from sub-miniature paintings on porcelain door knobs to a huge triptych of a magic sun-dragon, over nine feet long. He paints very smoothly with an eggshell finish. Everything is clear and precise with an almost classical use of perspective. His colours are bright, and lively and have an antique quality about them which suits the mystery in the paintings.

His paintings have been bought by several well-known collectors in

FERGUS HALL
McEve.
Oil/board, 14″ × 10″,
1977

126

Britain, Germany and the U.S.A. Stephen Manheimer in New York has a large collection. Nicholas Rothschild and Harry Hyams also have his paintings. Fergus Hall is definitely an acquired taste but like most acquired tastes he is relished by the connoisseur.

Before Fergus' exhibition in 1975, we were approached by Maurice Binder, the title designer for the James Bond films who wanted to commission Fergus to paint a set of tarot cards to be featured in the forth coming James Bond film *Live and Let Die*. Binder told us that the cards which had originally been designed by Salvador Dali were unsuitable and he thought that Fergus' images would be perfect. Under great pressure, Fergus completed the deck, possibly the most interesting tarot cards designed in recent years. The world-wide publicity and acclaim for the cards greatly enhanced Hall's reputation. He was also commissioned by the rock group "King Crimson" to do an album cover. The last Fergus

FERGUS HALL
Eight-Legged Horse.
11″ × 18″, 1976

Hall exhibition was in 1977. He works very slowly, and at the present time he is in Paisley, Scotland preparing a book, *Groundsel*, for Jonathan Cape, to be published early in 1982. We shall of course be exhibiting the original paintings which will appear in the book.

An interesting phenomenon which seems to have occurred during the 1970's is that a small school of self-taught Scottish fantasists, including Hall, has emerged and, although, individually their work is quite different, they seem to have something in common—an indefinable quality of magic linking them together. As these artists are not familiar with each other's work there is perhaps an hereditary gene of Scottish fantasy.

FERGUS HALL
St. Jerome.
Oil/board, 1974/75

opposite:
FERGUS HALL
The Elephant Hunter.
Oil/board, 20″ × 12″, 1977

X I X

Bernard Carter

Bernard Carter is a Londoner, was born in 1920, and, like many Londoners, the Thames is an integral part of his life. He lives with his wife, fabric collage artist Eugenie Alexander, in a magnificent Georgian house near the river at Greenwich. Bernard Carter's ambition to become a painter, began when he was a child at haberdasher's school. He was briefly at Goldsmith's College of Art, but this was interrupted by the Second World War, during which he served with the RAF in Egypt. On his return to civilian life he became an art teacher and in his leisure time began to teach, in his words, his "most difficult pupil"—himself. His natural affinity with the rivers and waterways of Britain made them a natural subject for his paintings. He enjoyed the quiet backwaters of the Thames and the almost forgotten canals which in their heyday, before the railways made them redundant, were vital to British commercial transportation. The goods would be drawn along the canals in long boats by horses, rather as they would pull a caravan. The boats were magnificent —the colors and designs were traditional, and everything on board, furniture, fabrics, and crockery, were all highly decorated—and some have recently been restored and are used as pleasure boats. Bernard Carter has made an intricate study of these barges and their environment—the tunnels, the towpaths, and the still water, the wildlife, owls and herons and the occasional foxes. He looked at the old pubs used by the "bargees" and their families which still exist by the side of the canals. He captures

every tiny detail in these lush paintings—his composition and application is meticulous.

    Carter first began to exhibit through the Arthur Jeffress Gallery and he also took part in the Royal Academy London Group Exhibition. His paintings have also hung in the London County Council exhibitions and in several prominent British and American collections. His exhibitions have been extensively reviewed, with articles appearing in the *Times, Sunday Telegraph, New York Times* and *Apollo Magazine,* plus his appear-

BERNARD CARTER
The Barge, Mary.
Oil/board, 1979

ances on several TV programmes. His paintings have been reproduced by Hallmark Cards, Shell Petroleum, British Petroleum and the International Publishing Company.

Bernard gave up teaching and joined the staff of the National Maritime Museum, Greenwich, as Keeper of Paintings. This gave him more opportunity to study marine paintings and subjects that were close to his heart, though he has recently retired to paint full-time. Over the years, his main subjects have been Britain's waterways or rivers. Some works include rather incongruous appearances such as *Camel in a punt,* where the camel sits sedately, floating down a magnificent, shaded, quiet, green backwater of the Thames and is propelled by an Oxford undergraduate. Several years ago, the *International Herald Tribune* said of Bernard

BERNARD CARTER
Cockerel.
Oil/board, 1979

Carter's work: "It is essentially rural painting, careful and contradictorily sophisticated. The paintings of English riverways emphasize a type of British painting that is currently neglected for more fashionable mannerisms, but sooner or later will come into its own and which is made so rightly and strangely that it is certain to endure." This prophecy has come true. . . .

opposite:
BERNARD CARTER
Pleasure Boat in Quiet Waters.
Oil/Board, 11″ × 10″, 1981

above:
BERNARD CARTER
Camel in a Punt.
Oil/board, 12″ × 15″, 1981

X X

Fred Aris

Fred Aris is unique among our painters; he has been showing with us for over fifteen years, during which time he has never had a one-man exhibition. Rarely are more than one of his paintings exhibited together. However, in spite of this lack of exposure, his work is in constant demand, both in Britain, the U.S. and in Europe. Although Aris himself might deny this, he is regarded by his admirers as something of a "mystery man." Lionel and I have known Fred since the mid-sixties, and when we are asked to talk about his background, we are still at a loss as how to fill in the few details we already know. The answer to this mystery is quite simple—Fred Aris has a quiet, retiring and gentle nature. He is a gentleman who, as an artist, wishes to remain anonymous and allow his work to speak for itself. He is not concerned with acclaim or media coverage and will not give interviews. His satisfaction comes from the act of painting and knowing that others appreciate his work. Although we often suggest a one-man show, he always declines, as he would not like the publicity and it would put him under pressure. He paints at a relaxed pace, and appears in the gallery about every three months with two paintings which he unveils and explains. After a few moments of small talk, he is presented with his up-to-date account, and leaves. If we wish to contact him for any reason—a commission, perhaps—we have to do so by telegram or letter, as he has no phone at home. Aris is dapper and almost as neat as his own paintings. There are few facts known about him:

he was born in South East London in 1934; besides painting, his interests are working in the cafe he inherited, and classical music.

 If I were to describe Fred's work in a word I should say "bold." The work has an affinity with American artists like Grant Wood and Andrew Wyeth—he shares their interest in a dust-free quality. His work reflects his own immaculate personality; there is never a blemish on the smooth surface, or a tonal gradation in his lively colours. Aris does not appear to have been influenced or even been particularly interested in the work of

FRED ARIS
Pigs in Bath.
Oil/board, 18″ × 22″, 1981

his fellow artists. He is entirely self-taught, and his work is immediately recognisable by his immaculate technique. The subject matter is generally of people or animals with enormous variety and sudden switches in time and place, like his study of three bowler-hatted Victorian street musicians, taken from a photograph that he spotted in a library book, to a couple of oriental children alongside a bonsai tree. His paintings of cats are celebrated and he was one of our earliest painters of this theme, but now this has become almost too overworked as a subject for him.

In *Two Persons at a Green Baize Table*, we see what looks like a full-colour photograph taken years before colour photography. The two

FRED ARIS
Owl and Pussycat.

opposite:
FRED ARIS
Chef.
Oil/board, 20″ × 24″, 1971

138

people, who are obviously based on Oscar Wilde and his friend "Bosie," Lord Alfred Douglas, are caught during one of their less friendly moments, perhaps seated in the lounge of a fashionable seaside hotel, irritated by the lack of service. The use of a bright, pink background matching Wilde's carnation, is brilliant, and the simplicity of the composition enhances the riveting stares of Oscar and "Bosie."

In 1978, Aris painted a pair of oil paintings for our Christmas *Jonah and the Whale* exhibition—there were around sixty paintings by all our

opposite:
FRED ARIS
Oscar and Bosie.
Oil/board

FRED ARIS
Jonah and the Whale.
Oil/board, 20″ × 24″, 1978

141

artists on the same theme. Aris made two contributions because he wanted to show Jonah as an ancient during a violent storm, being tossed by the sea into the jaws of a giant whale. The second painting shows Jonah emerging several thousand years later, from the mouth of the same whale, somewhere along the beach at Brighton. It is a calm, sunny day and Jonah, rejuvenated after his stay inside, is waving happily goodbye to his companion. He is appropriately wearing a brand new Saville Row suit complete with the accouterments of a British stockbroker. It is a delightfully humourous and surreal composition.

The Royal Crescent at Bath is a more recent painting. It is dated from spring 1981, when we exhibited at the annual Bath Arts Fair and asked our painters to paint something appropriate. Perhaps the most splendid Georgian architecture to be found in this gorgeous Somerset town is the famous and totally unspoilt Royal Crescent. This we see painstakingly portrayed by Aris, with the casual addition of an elderly gentleman rather contradictorily dressed in a battered hat and shabby, full-length, green coat over a new pinstriped suit, leading a large and friendly sow across the road by a rope. As if this were not strange enough, there is a squadron of flying pigs appearing in formation over the Crescent behind.

In 1978, film producer, Michael Deeley, and his wife, commissioned Fred Aris to paint their tomcat. Aris always takes a completely free hand when he paints a subject suggested to him. The Deeleys were delighted with their portrait. Using the Edward Lear poem "The Owl and the Pussycat," Aris had depicted their huge tomcat in a "pea green boat" with an owl, strumming a guitar. In description this painting may sound banal, but when seen, all Fred Aris' paintings are as lively and buoyant as the pea green boat!

XXI

Elizabeth Allen

Londoner Elizabeth Allen was one of a family of seventeen children. She had severe spine and leg disablements from birth and due to these physical deformities, she was taught to sew at a very early age by her father, himself a self-employed tailor. This poor child born in the late Victorian era was destined to spend her life working as a seamstress. Unable to work normally, she was lonely and without a chance of romance. When she was quite young she did have a few friends but they gradually disappeared. Elizabeth ended her long life in virtual isolation, still sewing, but no longer as a seamstress. In her middle age, with a little money she had saved, she left London and went to live alone in a little iron house close to a thickly wooded area near Biggin Hill, Kent. This area was famous as a Battle of Britain airfield during the Second World War. Although Elizabeth lived virtually as a recluse, she did have the occasional visitor and in fact became friends with a local girl who attended art school. The girl was intrigued to find that Elizabeth worked on quilted and embroidered pictures. These exquisitely sewn pieces were of various subjects, sometimes quite bizarre. Often biblical stories were depicted with a kind of sublime passivity. Her colours were as rich and as expensive as Edwardian candies. The girl borrowed a few of these pieces and showed them to her tutor, who, in turn, brought them into the Portal. We appreciated the work and considered exhibiting it, but, as we were offered it through a third party who was obviously financially interested and expected more than we could offer, we suggested our old friend

ELIZABETH ALLEN
The Dove.
Patchwork

opposite:
ELIZABETH ALLEN
The Artist in Rags.
Patchwork, 11″ × 15½″

Andreas Kalman of the Crane Kalman Gallery who was able to make a deal. Apart from this, we prefer to have direct contact with the artist. By the time Elizabeth was recognised as an artist, she was a very old lady and unable to enjoy her brief success. She died only one year after Kalman exhibited her work and never learned of her acclaim abroad, especially in New York, Los Angeles and Germany.

Although I never met her, I am told that Elizabeth Allen's gentle charm echoed her embroideries and it is obviously this charm that diffuses the nighmarish quality in many of her works. As in the dream of Nebuchadnezzar, in which the trouserless monarch crawls out of a cage watched by a horned figure looming in the background, this is a typical dream-story and suggests the innocence of childhood, not the sophistication of mysticism.

ELIZABETH ALLEN
*Babylon Riding on
the Great Dragon.*
Patchwork, 16″ × 20″, ca. 1950

XXII

Kit Williams

Of all the Portal painters, Kit Williams is truly one of a very select breed—an international artist. This might come as something of a surprise to art connoisseurs, as most people equate artists with writers, musicians, filmmakers, people who often become internationally known figures within a short space of time. Artists sometimes become national figures during their lifetimes, but usually their fame remains parochial. I often ask our clients to name six living, truly international artists from their own countries, and more often than not they can only mention two or three before giving up. There are, of course, a number of artists who are internationally known to collectors, although not necessarily to the general public. Some British artists, such as David Hockney, Henry Moore, Graham Sutherland, Ben Nicholson, and Peter Blake, have become internationally known, but other national figures who have become household names, such as L. S. Lowry and Beryl Cook are not so widely known outside Britain. Even in the U.S.A., only a handful of names—Andy Warhol, Andrew Wyeth, Norman Rockwell—have become widely known outside the confines of the art world.

Media exposure for artists is so irregular that the public never has enough of an opportunity to remember their names. The name of an author or a popular musician or filmmaker becomes much better known because their products are seen by millions. The well-known axiom that an artist is better-known after he is dead, is sadly too often true. The chance to enjoy an international reputation does not happen for many excellent artists. This is an unfortunate situation which still exists, despite the modern media.

Kit Williams, who is now 35 years old, is already known to millions of people throughout the world. This phenomena has occurred because he has combined two of his many talents—painting and writing. His book, *Masquerade*, has made his paintings available to over two million readers in fourteen different countries and has brought him an international reputation in less than two years.

First and foremost, Kit Williams is a superb artist who conceived the idea of *Masquerade*, published by Jonathan Cape, London 1979, by painting a series of sixteen exquisitely intricate pictures through which he weaves a story. Characteristic of his agile mind, he devised a puzzle which requires the reader to look very closely into each one of the paintings for clues to a buried treasure, a magnificent golden hare set with jewels, made by Kit and buried by him somewhere in Britain. While the idea may be considered something of a gimmick by some people, Kit has successfully solved the problem shared by many fellow artists. He has insured that people look very closely indeed at his paintings. The familiar cliché about the small acorn and mighty oak tree is applicable to Kit's emergence as an artist.

Lionel Levy visited the John Moores exhibition at the Walker Art Gallery, Liverpool during 1972 and noticed a small and very intense painting of a naked girl, partially obscured by a large black bird, against the background of a Morris Minor car, in a rural setting. Lionel spoke to the museum curator and was given a forwarding address for the artist— Christopher Williams. When I was shown the small illustration in the catalogue, I agreed that the work was extraordinary, a blend of rural surrealism painted with infinite care and painstaking detail. After a while, we managed to contact Williams. It was difficult because he was living in a caravan with his current wife, Helen, also a painter, and they were in the process of moving to rooms above a small village post office in Bedfordshire.

Kit's subsequent appearance at the gallery was almost as startling as his paintings. He is of medium height and slightly built. Most of his face is covered by a dark, bushy beard and he has a heavy mop of hair. His eyes (once seen, never forgotten) are large, serious, brown and point in opposite directions. Complementing these physical attributes was the thickest woolen, multi-coloured suit we had ever seen. He was also wearing hand-painted, green leather shoes. Before showing us his paint-

KIT WILLIAMS
Orrery.
Oil/canvas,
mixed fruit woods,
brass, 23″ diameter,
1975

KIT WILLIAMS
Village Cricket.
Oil/canvas,
marquetry frame

ings, Christopher Williams explained how he had sheared the sheep, dyed, processed, and woven the wool, to make this fantastic suit of which he was obviously very proud. The few paintings he showed us were extraordinary examples of super-realism painted with meticulous precision in jewel-like colours. Each painting was surrounded by a beautifully crafted wooden marquetry frame, inlaid with symbols, thus becoming an integral part of the work. Nature was the predominant subject and although the figures were in modern dress, the effect and atmosphere was timeless and mysterious. At a nearby coffee shop, Kit told us something of his background.

He was born and raised in Tenterden, Kent, the second son of a bicycle salesman. His grandfather had been a master gunsmith and Kit believed that he had inherited some of his skills. It was not until he joined the Royal Navy that he began to make use of these skills. During long voyages he would sketch and make small wood carvings. On his discharge from the Navy, he decided to become an artist and, with his natural intuition, he taught himself to use oils and develop his wood carving. He began to use many different techniques, and soon became proficient in the use of precious and semi-precious metals, gemstones and woods. The techniques and tools he used for fashioning the materials were antique

150

and traditional. He felt that it was necessary to teach himself the roots before indulging in more modern methods. Once he develops a skill he becomes confident, rarely making a mistake.

At the outset, Kit was obviously limited by lack of finances. Living with his wife, he earned money by a series of varied jobs—steeplejack, TV aerial mechanic, and, uncharacteristically, as a computer operator, another self-taught skill!

Sometimes during the late sixties, the Williamses in their caravan were parked on the East Coast and to amuse themselves one evening, put messages in soda bottles and threw them out to sea. The messages gave Kit's family's telephone number and asked the recipient to contact them. Although he did not realise it at the time, this game charted the course of his future, for, some months later, they received a message from a man who had found a bottle on a beach several miles away and had contacted Kit's family. They eventually met a rather seedy man who claimed to be a fellow artist and to have found the bottle. He was invited to join the Williamses and initially he was a welcome guest. However, after some time, despite hints from his hosts, he began to outstay his welcome, although he did prove to be a starting link in the chain of Kit's success. During his stay with Kit he collected some entry forms from a London gallery for the John Moores exhibition. When he left, Kit found a form and decided on an exhibition as a final attempt to gain recognition by entering a painting. He was somewhat reluctant, as his only previous exhibition at the Bristol Art Centre had hardly attracted anyone and none of his paintings were sold. He had decided at that point to forgo the fame and fortune of the gallery world. However, as a result of this strange sequence of events, he was accepted for the Moores and spotted by my partner.

We planned an exhibition of about twenty paintings and I drove to Bedfordshire to see more of his work. Once again, I was quite staggered by the quality, which was comparable in detail to some of the finest old masters, a latter day Breugel or Hieronymous Bosch.

At the first exhibition of Kit's work in 1973, his paintings were a revelation to serious collectors who were obviously very impressed with the quality. All these paintings were sold with the month. Elton John snapped up a beauty of an English cricket match. British news columnist, Felicity Green, theatre impressario, Michael White, and noted collector, Gillian Kean, were among the first British buyers. Abroad, they were

bought for the Muller collection in Germany. There was even a surprising call from Saudi Arabia, a place where contemporary art collectors are very scarce indeed; the discerning Mr. Hage Ali had seen Kit's work reproduced in a British newspaper and agreed to buy a painting over the phone. Two noted collectors in New York and Connecticut were Stephen Manheimer and Victor Fassler.

Obviously, Kit and his wife needed a more permanent base, with room to work. At that time, we owned a tiny artisan's eighteenth-century cottage in the Cotswolds, Gloucestershire, Although this was an ideal

KIT WILLIAMS
Flora.
Oil/canvas,
marquetry frame,
14½″ × 17″

opposite:
KIT WILLIAMS
Advancing Ripe Harvest.
Oil/canvas,
inlaid wood frame,
20½″ × 15½″, 1973

153

weekend haven, situated on the slopes of lush green valley divided by a lake, we rarely used it. I therefore suggested to Kit that we should make an exchange of the cottage for his next exhibition of paintings. He was as enchanted as I was with this backwater in the rolling Gloucestershire countryside, and agreed. He built a minute studio onto the cottage and worked steadily for the forthcoming show. Perhaps the greatest influence in his new paintings was this magic "patch" of countryside. The nearby small town was a relic of a bygone age—it had seen its heyday during the early nineteenth-century Industrial Revolution, but had sunk into a decline since that time. The rural, water-driven fabric mills, built of grey-brown Cotswold stone, were shuttered and abandoned. Most of the local population now commuted to larger towns for work. The little town and valley was sleepy with a soft and gentle atmosphere. Kit was quickly immersed in this strange, almost medieval place which soon became such an inspiration to his painting; the spirits of the seasons, and the myths and legends of ancient Britain all became entwined with his interest in astronomy and nature.

Kit used local wood, which was easy to find, for his frames, and he quickly gained knowledge of the nearby fields, hedgerows, woods and animal life. Badgers, stoats and a variety of birds all came into his life, but perhaps what attracted him above all was the mad "March" hare, a traditional symbol in English folklore.

His second successful exhibition featured paintings as well as the most incredible objects, like a wonderful "orrery," a medieval, astrological instrument made of inlaid woods with a circular painting of intertwined figures, and a polished brass song-thrush as a pointer, which was bought by the American film producer Elliott Kastner.

Kit began to concentrate his thoughts around a series of nature paintings with the Hare as the central figure. Around this time, I was en route for a weekend break in Wales with the British publisher, Tom Maschler, of Jonathan Cape. Driving along the motorway, I suddenly turned onto a minor road. Tom remarked that we were off-course, and I told him he was being hijacked to visit Kit Williams. Maschler was obviously very impressed with Kit and his work, and when we left the cottage he remarked that, splendid as Kit's work was, he could not see a book in it. Knowing Kit quite well I suggested that Tom leave it entirely to him. Within a few weeks, Tom had received a synopsis of Kit's idea for a book based on his imaginative paintings of the Hare. Later it was agreed that a gold Hare, set with precious stones, should be buried, and clues to its whereabouts should be concealed in the paintings.

The sixteen, now world-famous paintings were accompanied by a fascinating text. *Masquerade* was published in October 1979, and we had an exhibition of the original paintings at the same time. As before, the response was immediate and despite the obvious increase in the price of his work, the sixteen paintings were quickly sold to leading international collectors. Likewise, the response to the book was almost explosive. Within a few weeks, Kit's work was known throughout Britain and he appeared regularly on television and radio interviews. There were also major articles in the *Observer* and the *Sunday Times*, Britain's two most prestigious Sunday newspapers. Several Kit Williams treasure clubs were organised and he was inundated with communications by eager searchers of all ages. Some were submitting quite preposterous ideas and Kit was soon receiving an enormous amount of mail by every post.*

When *Masquerade* was published in New York by Schocken Books, late in 1980, Kit's mail trebled within a few weeks and the book quickly became a U.S. best seller. Kit and I visited New York at the time and he remained in America to appear before audiences throughout the country, signing his books and giving TV, radio and newspaper interviews galore.

He returned to Gloucestershire after a very exhausting but exciting month. By now the book is published in most European and Scandinavian countries and is about to be published in Israel and Japan. Approximately two million books have been sold worldwide and people are still searching for the elusive treasure. People still wonder if the treasure will ever be found, but no one knows—it does exist exactly as Kit has explained and can be found with the right combination of will and skills by anyone anywhere.

Before the appearance of *Masquerade*, Kit and Helen were divorced. Both have since remarried. Kit now lives a few hundred yards away from the old cottage, in a similar, but somewhat larger old house surrounded by a wild garden and rushing brook. The fame and financial improvement in Kit's life have changed his way of life very little. He and Elayne enjoy comfort but do not need luxury. He is very generous and loyal to his old friends, and although he could well afford to live in exotic climes, he has no intention of leaving his beloved Gloucestershire. Despite the fact that odd people arrive at his cottage at inconvenient times with solutions, he is

*Editor's Note: The MASQUERADE rabbit was finally found in March 1982.

KIT WILLIAMS
Song of Summer
Oil/canvas, marquetry frame
12″ × 12″

patient and hospitable. It is perhaps because of these unwanted interruptions that he has built himself a small studio workshop where he continues with his new series of paintings, and a book due for publication around 1983. This promises to be at least as spectacular as *Masquerade*.

During the next year or so, a book about Kit's multi-faceted work is being planned by a prominent British art historian and critic. *Masquerade* is now an established classic and Kit himself feels that it will eventually become a kind of late 20th century *Alice in Wonderland*. Above everything else, Kit Williams is an artist and will continue to paint. He feels that the books are the first stage in establishing his career as an artist. I think that it is appropriate to conclude this chapter on Kit's work with a quotation by him from our 1977 catalogue in which he says: "This is the third London exhibition of my work and it should be evident that the marriage between the engineer and painter has been consummated. I have been concerning myself with the concept of symbolism. We live in an age where, by way of the media, everyone has a little knowledge of the symbolism used by all the great civilisations, but a concise knowledge of none. When Celtic, Egyptian, or Renaissance man wished to communicate visually he had a whole symbolic vocabulary to draw upon. He worked within a discipline. Occasionally, one is confronted by things that seem to communicate directly. Instead of trying to fathom the true meaning, I have allowed myself to be taken over by the image itself. It does seem at times that symbols, far from aiding communication, serve more to confuse the issue, leaving the images themselves to reign supreme."

XXIII

George James Kirk

Nowadays, it is a rare occurrence for a genuine primitive artist of considerable vision to surface. Such an artist was George James Kirk. He was born on John Street, Nuneaton, Leicestershire, in 1901, and he died in the same house in 1974. Shortly after his death, a friend of the family, Pam Evans, helped to clear the house and noticed several paintings and wood carvings among Kirk's frugal effects. She brought these to the attention of a friend of hers, a local school teacher, Penny Johnson, who was immediately struck by their quality. She brought them for us to see. This resulted in Kirk's posthumous exhibition. Perhaps the artist was happy in his own way. We can only hope so, as his life was as uneventful as it was unnoticed.

The Kirk family was from the romantic-sounding town of Ashby de la Zouche, close to Nuneaton, where his grandfather owned a chandler's shop. George's niece, Mrs. Downs, the only surviving member of the Kirk family, was able to supply details about his life, as she knew him as a child. She told Pam and Penny that, due to a severe case of diptheria when he was only three, he was left partially deaf. Then, at twelve, he contracted Bright's disease and shortly afterwards, suffered a personality change. The symptoms described sound somewhat akin to schizophrenia.

GEORGE JAMES KIRK
Devel Water.
Oil/wood, 14½″ × 11½″

He became very withdrawn for the rest of his life. She said that he was a childlike man although not childish. He lived with his parents and, after their death, lived alone in the small house. Neighbours and locals were polite about him, but suggested that he was never quite "right" in the head. Nevertheless, he was a working man, mainly a rough carpenter who made pit props for the local coal mine, Newdigate Colliery. He was a

familiar figure for many years on his bicycle riding to and from work. In fact, cycling was one of his few pleasures. On his days off he often rode around the local countryside. As far as is known, he had never been on holiday or visited Scotland or Ireland or seen the ocean—all subjects that feature in his paintings. Living alone, he kept to himself. At the age of seventy he became seriously ill, though he never complained or told anyone. In 1974 a visiting doctor diagnosed cancer and although he was virtually incapable of looking after himself during the last few months of his life, he does seem to have carried on with his painting. Unfortunately, the house was in such a terrible state that many paintings and carvings were burned by the neighbours when clearing it out. It is fortunate that Pam Evans happened to notice and save the ones that she did.

It is impossible to say when or how Kirk took up painting. One can only surmise that as a lonely and somewhat inarticulate man he came to it by instinct. His work is crude, the paint is cheap household enamel paint. Like Alfred Wallis and James Dixon, he seems to have painted any flat surface that came to hand. We find the shapes of teatrays, boxes, mirrors, door panels and some crude, wooden carvings. Some of his carvings were embellished by grooves burned into the wood with a hot poker. He uses bright, strong colours; black, green and red predominate. Most of the subjects range from early nineteenth-century tea clippers to poignant meetings between kilted Scottish soldiers and their lassies. There are constantly repeated farewell scenes from the First World War, which makes one wonder if he did at one period befriend a young lady and retain romantic memories for the rest of his days.

After the successful exhibition, I kept a nice little carving of a cyclist (probably himself). It appeared that he once plucked up courage to show his work to the Nuneaton Art Gallery but like fellow miner artist C.W. Brown, he was turned down. This is a great shame, as he deserved the recognition that only came after his death.

GEORGE JAMES KIRK
The Campbells Are Coming.
Oil/wood, 12″ × 13″

overleaf:
GEORGE JAMES KIRK
Sleeping Man with Dog.
Oil/wood, 12″ × 13″

XXIV

P. J. Crook

Pamela Crook was born in the genteel Gloucestershire town of Cheltenham in 1945, but her paintings certainly give no indication of this background. As with some other "self-taught" artists mentioned in this book, I use the label metaphorically. She attended the Gloucestershire College of Art for nearly four years, but the knowledge of painting she gained during these years bears no relation to her present style. This is perhaps because of her choice of studies during her time at art school—textile design, print making, etching and lithography. These multiple interests enabled her to earn a living in London for a few years. She was in partnership designing jewellry and pop art posters as a sideline. She also worked as an industrial designer of toys for which she received an award from the Council of Industrial Design.

In 1969, Pam married, and went to live with her husband in Weston-Super-Mare, a Somerset seaside town close to Bristol where she continued with her freelance work. In 1971 her daughter, Henrietta, was born and in 1974, her son, Nathan. In between these events, she began to paint her very idiosyncratic pictures. Since then, she has developed her extraordinary style of painting and has brought up her two children.

P. J. Crook's work is immediately distinguishable by the frames (or lack of frames). The painting continues onto the full width of the specially designed heavy-stepped moulding. The steps become an integral part of the perspective. This unique style that she has developed gives her paintings a wonderful trompe l'oeil effect, and her subject matter is strange and intriguing.

Her pictures range in size from an almost miniature 4 inch square to others that are 5 feet by 4 feet. She sometimes uses a half-box for a painting, so that there is a painted inner surface, for an almost theatrical effect. To say her subject matter is strange would be an inadequate description—they exude a quality of eeriness not unlike that of Victorian wax dolls. Appropriately, *Parade*, a small painting of two rows of stern-faced nannies, is set in a Victorian nursery. Standing on a black and white chequer-board floor is a tiny golden-haired child, wearing what

P. J. CROOK
The Brides.
Acrylic/canvas, 1979/80

opposite:
P. J. CROOK,
Parade.
Acrylic/canvas,
8″ × 10″, 1979/80

appears to be diapers. He is inspecting the nannies like a general inspecting his troops. In the arched background we see the child's rocking horse, while overhead are vintage electric lamp shades, their yellow bulbs sending shafts of light downward. The whole painting creates a three-dimensional effect of depth and light and shadow. The colours which P. J. Crook favours are blues and greys and a muted pink. They are unvarnished, flat and almost faded which again adds to the strange, timeless atmosphere.

The Brides, a large, quite brilliant surrealist composition, is an outdoor scene where shadows are cast over the frame section. The idea of a docile

zebra among the white-gowned brides with their bright red posies, seen within an avenue of phallic trees, is quite worthy of Giorgio de Chirico. What links all surrealist painters are their unlikely juxtapositions, placing strange objects in mundane settings or vice versa. Though not necessarily directly influenced, P. J. Crook is definitely related to the surrealists.

In another large canvas, *Time and Time Again*, we see what might almost have been a Magritte, executed in a skillful and interesting way. It is a superb example of her originality. She depicts two figures and a dog, within a simply decorated room and, by an ingenious arrangement of mirrors, doors and objects, we see them reversed and reversed, to infinity. The lamp overhead is beamed to leave the upper corners of the room in shadow. The picture is painted mainly in blue-green and pink. This fantastic composition was first exhibited at the Royal Academy Summer Exhibition in 1981 and is now in the Stephen Manheimer collection, New York.

P. J. Crook's career, considering that she has only been painting for five years, is as remarkable as her work. She has already gained a number of first prizes and been highly commended in sixteen different exhibitions. She has shown and been accepted three times at the Royal Academy Summer Exhibitions, a very difficult exhibition to get into, as they have over ten thousand entries each year. She is also well-known in the West of England Academy exhibitions and on Westward Television. Her exhibition in 1980 was her first one-man show, and sold completely. Pam, currently working on her second Portal show, is a most extraordinary artist with a very promising future.

P. J. Crook
Time and Time Again.
Acrylic/canvas, 1981

X X V

Peter Heard

If there is an inopportune time and place for the birth of a child, Peter Heard's parents found a choice one—London, 1939! One can almost feel the veil of gloom descending on the capital as Big Ben struck eleven on the 3rd September.

It has been said that wartime babies were healthy and athletic and Peter Heard appears to endorse this. He has enjoyed a lifelong interest in English sports. This is combined with a humourous interest in its more eccentric participants. A happy and contented individual, he is married, with two daughters, and lives in a village in Essex, close to London.

Heard is, by profession, a civil engineer who specialises in building bridges. Always interested in sketching and painting, he has gradually devoted more and more of his spare time to this absorbing pastime.

Around 1970, Peter began using oils and, formulating his own style, gradually developed a high finish to his naive realism. He uses brilliant, startling colours which leap at you from his glossy paintings. The figures in these paintings are usually very prominent and well in the foreground, often wearing period headgear and clothing. Peter's two Portal exhibitions since 1978 have been entitled *England's Green and Pleasant Land* and *The English at Their Sports and Pastimes*. The paintings have enormous appeal and, although he was virtually unknown before his first show, some of the *Sports* series were used by Felix Rosenstiel to be published as prints and as a calendar for 1982. There were twenty-eight different sports depicted and, apart from the obvious ones, some distinctly

PETER HEARD
Tabbit's Shop. Oil/wood panel, 1977

PETER HEARD, *Hiker and Sheep*.
Oil/wood panel, 17″ × 14″, 1977

opposite: PETER HEARD, *Train Spotting*.
Oil/wood panel, 17″ × 14″, 1980

170

Peter Heard.

esoteric and not quite so sporting ones—British butterfly collecting, pigeon fancying, and the childlike, but nevertheless very serious pastime, model train set arranging. We see an intense, albeit eccentric, elderly and moustachioed Englishman wearing a period railway guard's hat whilst manuevering his train set which covers the entire floor around him in a semi-detached suburban villa. Most of the male characters in the paintings sport moustaches and rather sombre expressions. The ladies are sensibly hatted and often, like the gentlemen, wear straw panamas. Some people wear monocles or pince-nez and they obviously all take their pastimes very seriously. Although the paintings have a contemporary feel, Peter Heard manages to evoke an atmosphere of an earlier era with the tiny village shops with their alluring coloured enamel signs, the smooth, lush bowling greens with their octogenarian participants, the small, pretty churches, flagpoles bristling with Union Jacks, gleaming touring cars and the various pets which appear in unexpected places. Peter Heard has an easy and immediate international appeal and we are looking forward to his new series on English village life in 1982.

XXVI

Martin Leman

Another Londoner born and bred is Martin Leman. Martin was born in 1934. His father was a fruit porter at Covent Garden, and he clearly remembers watching his father at work in the famous and colourful London market,which, although carefully preserved, is used only for a somewhat contrived "crafts" community. The fresh and vivid colours of the fruit, which arrived daily from home and abroad, obviously strongly impressed Martin because, when, as a young man, he started painting, he looked to these strong colours for his palette.

After leaving school, Leman served a short time in the Army. He was released after two years to take up an apprenticeship as a typographer, an occupation which he worked at for several years. He filled his spare time playing chess, at which he is exceptionally accomplished, editing his own magazine, *Arcade*, and, of course, painting. Toward the end of the sixties, painting became his main occupation and he became a full-time artist.

A lifelong love of cats ensured that many of his earliest works would have feline subjects, sometimes as the predominant feature. Leman is now world-famous for his cats, which are bold and sensuous. He is one of the finest British cat painters.

It is, however, his lesser-known compositions that I find of greater interest. They are comparable, and often unintentionally similar, to those brassy portraits of sexy ladies of my own favourite American, self-taught painter, Morris Hirschfield. These happy, blousy young women are seen during personal and often intimate moments. They are always portrayed

nude or very scantily clad in rather claustrophobic interiors, often their bedrooms. They are preparing themselves for an event which requires a careful toilette and are sometimes attended by maids, dressed appropriately. There are large mirrors in which we see a multitude of views of madame's curvaceous form. The chaise lounges are littered with flimsy clothing and cheap jewelery. Perhaps a ginger cat curls up moodily on the floor or peeps out from under the bed. In one such scene, somewhat less intimate,

MARTIN LEMAN
Fat Black Cat.
Oil/wood panel,
15″ × 18″, 1981

174

we see three perky young ladies, obviously entertainers, who are practising for a local musical show or perhaps a cheap night club act. The topless lady (apart from a man's bowtie) is seated at a piano. Her sisters, behind the piano, sport a banjo and are ready to sing along. The unusual pattern of veneers on the piano and the rather loud, floral wallpaper add to this very "jazzy" composition. Leman's careful paintwork and "glossy flat" finish ensure the success of the composition. Sometimes Leman's paintings are distinctly erotic, but never lewd. There are paintings of bouquets in vases which are decorated with intricate landscapes, each separate flower carefully groomed for stardom. Occasionally, and rather in the manner of John Deakin, he will surprise us with a glorious ship on a moonlit, tropical ocean, in full sail and incongruously displaying a Union Jack. Or sometimes a Pop Art dish of cookies and ice cream with other weight watchers' enemies depicted in glorious technicolour.

Now, after twelve years as a professional artist, Leman is very close to being internationally known. He has exhibited extensively in Europe and the United States, where his work hangs in several noted collections of self-taught artists. He has had four, highly successful one-man shows at the Portal Gallery. Since 1979, his three books *Comic and Curious Cats*, *The Book of Beasts*, and *Star Cats*, all published by Victor Gollancz, have had combined sales well into six figures and are still selling well.

MARTIN LEMAN
Dressing.
Oil/wood panel

XXVII
Beryl Cook

Beryl Cook's personality is, like the people in her paintings, a little larger than life. Like Toby Lyon, she was a "jazz baby," born in 1926 in Egham, Surrey. Her family moved to Reading, in Berkshire, where she attended the Kendrick School, and showed none of her future artistic talent. Her first job was as a very junior junior in a local insurance office, but, by the time she was seventeen, the family had moved to London and Beryl managed to persuade them to disregard Noel Coward's stern advice and allow her to go on the stage. Her enthusiasm at that age matches her enthusiasm today and she soon netted a show girl's part in a touring production of *The Gypsy Princess*. Unfortunately, even her bubbling personality could not keep her in work, and before long she joined a dress manufacturer as a showroom model. This "on display" era of Beryl Tansley's life toned down somewhat in 1946, when her mother and sister, Freda, bought a house with an adjoining tea garden overlooking the Thames at Hampton Court, where they served English afternoon teas. Romantically, she soon married her boyfriend since school days, John Cook, then an officer in the Merchant Navy. Perhaps not quite so romantically, both John and Beryl fell into the river during their wedding party at the tea rooms, no doubt with the assistance of a little liquid refreshment! This unintentional baptism into married life seems to have been a special blessing, as today, after thirty-five years, they are as happy as honeymooners. Their son, John, was born in 1950 and a few years later John Sr. gave up his maritime career to live with his family in Essex and manage a pub. However, John soon decided that a change of air might do

BERYL COOK
Keyhole.
Oil/board,
24" × 24", 1981

BERYL COOK
Jackson Square.
Oil/board, 1980

them all good and they went to live in Southern Rhodesia, where he worked in the motor industry and Beryl took a series of jobs in a variety of offices. It was at this time that Beryl first picked up a paint brush—actually like James Lloyd, it was from a child's painting set. She so enjoyed teaching young John to paint that she commandeered his set and started to paint her own pictures of native women and local market scenes. Like many other self-taught painters, she felt the bug bite and soon returned the toy set to young John and bought herself a more serious set. Her work improved by degrees and she begun to feel more confident.

After a few years in Africa, the Cooks moved back to Cornwall, buying a picturesque cottage on the harbour at Looe, a tiny fishing village. Like the primitive, Alfred Wallis, who lived and died nearby, Beryl took to painting in oils on wood or scraps of cardboard, and her work soon covered the walls of their house.

The Cook family then moved to Plymouth Hoe in the late sixties. John Sr. had settled into a managerial job with a major motor company and during the summer months, Beryl ran a holiday boarding house.

All her life, Beryl had been a keen observer of human types and, as a landlady, had a great opportunity to study Homo sapiens. With her impish sense of humour, these human "types" became the obvious subjects for the paintings which she worked on throughout the winter months. Beryl hung her paintings all through the house and, although admired by everyone, she still did not consider exhibiting them. In fact, even now, she cannot bear to part with her work and finds it difficult to paint without some of her paintings on the walls around her.

Beryl and John would often visit their local pub which featured a gay bar and local drag acts. These "turns" were an important source of inspiration to her as an artist. She is fond of homosexuals and paints them with kindness and humour. Her meticulous observation of amusing, often amorous situations keeps appearing in her new work, her colours and forms becoming bolder. The paintings have a less caricatured quality, and are blossoming into unique social commentaries while remaining always full of fun.

The paintings are comparable to those of the famous, seaside, post-card artist, Donald McGill. All kinds of people, in all kinds of situations, appear in Beryl's work. Immaculately dressed ladies play bowls in a picture entitled *Sabotage*, with one lady "goosing" another as she bends to

BERYL COOK
Chinese Restaurant.
Oil/board, 24″ × 24″, 1981

opposite:
BERYL COOK
Two Greek Gods.

182

B. Cook

play her shot. There are fat, jolly nudes, groups of Salvation Army people, and even paintings of fairies in a dell. Beryl's artistic confidence grew, until she would have a go at anything, except selling her work. It was not until 1975 that she finally relented and allowed an antique dealer friend to try a few in his shop. She was amazed and delighted when he returned in a few days with a bunch of "fivers."

Bernard Samuels of the Plymouth Art Centre contacted her, and with some difficulty, persuaded her to hold an exhibition of seventy-five paintings. This locally organised exhibition was the springboard for Beryl's forthcoming success. It was noticed by the *Sunday Times* colour supplement writer, Allen Saddler, who wrote a major article for the magazine, which included a full colour cover.

Lionel and I agreed that her work was exciting, and a Portal exhibition was arranged in due course. Prior to our show, Beryl was seen at the Alexander Gallery in Bristol, and later at the Whitechapel Gallery, London. After the first Portal exhibition which was completely sold out within a few days, London art critic, Edward Lucie-Smith, wrote a major article in the *Evening Standard*, entitled, "Mrs Cook's Flash of Genius," in which he considers her a worthy successor of Hogarth and "the nicest thing to happen to British painting for years."

Beryl Cook's paintings are a source of genuine pleasure to a great many people, many of whom have never considered looking at paintings before. Her prints, and reproductions of her paintings as cards, have endeared her to the British public at large. Lionel Levy introduced her work to the publishers, John Murray, in 1978 who, together with Gallery Five, published *The Works*, an immediate best seller which has gone into several editions. This was followed in 1980 by *Private View* acclaimed by almost all the British press and again a best seller. The same year, she did a children's book for Collins publishers, *Seven Years and a Day*, with a text by Colette O'Hare. Children have been as keen on Beryl's work as adults. Late in 1981, the *One-Man Show* was published and is another success, as were the original paintings which all sold in an exhibition to coincide with publication. While the media clamours to interview Beryl, she remains something of an enigma. Although she is a happy individual, when it comes to discussing her own work, she is shy and reticent. To get her in front of a microphone or a TV camera requires a great deal of persuasion. Perhaps it is this endearing modesty and shyness beneath the jolly exterior which gives her work such an obviously sincere quality.

XXVIII

Patrick

It was only after his first visit to the Portal in 1967 that Glasgow born John Byrne adopted the inexplicable nickname "Patrick," with which he used to sign his paintings. Prior to his re-christening, John Byrne had sent us a small parcel containing a small painting on board entitled *Old Man in Panama Hat*, accompanied by a note telling us that it was the work of his seventy-two year old father, a newspaper seller from Glasgow. We were very impressed with this loosely painted primitive and replied to Byrne, Jr., asking to see more of his father's work. A few weeks later several more small paintings arrived, all good, if somewhat reminiscent of Alfred Wallis. It was clear that the subject matter was somewhat contrived; however, the quality was excellent, so we suggested that he visit us next time he was in London.

A tall, dark, rather gaunt man in his late twenties, arrived and introduced himself as John Byrne. He was quietly spoken with a strong Scottish brogue and piercing dark eyes. During the ensuing conversation we sensed that there was something a little contrived about his work. Eventually, and with some embarrassment, he told us that the paintings were his, but because he felt it was part of the make-up of a successful primitive to be an elderly person of humble origins, he had invented that story about his dad. An unusual, somewhat unethical approach, but it resulted in our meeting a brilliant artist who was not a septogenarian.

Patrick, at a very early age, had enrolled at the Glasgow School of Art. In 1963 he was awarded a travelling scholarship to Italy. His wanderings around Italy, particularly in the early medieval town of Assisi, were a

permanent influence on his artistic style. He was deeply impressed by the bold, primitive quality of the frescoes by Giotto and paintings by Duccio and Cimabue. Duccio was also a great favourite of the self-taught artist James Lloyd, who copied an illustration he saw of Duccio's *St. George and the Dragon*.

On returning to Scotland, Byrne found work first as a designer in television, and later as a designer in the carpet industry. In 1967, he painted what he considers to be his first "Patrick" painting, a small work, measuring six by four inches and painted in gouache on white card, of the man in a panama hat holding a bunch of flowers. John told us that until that time, he had felt unsettled and was unable to think of painting as a career, with a wife and four children to support. After reading a feature in

PATRICK
Child with a Lion.
Gouache/paper,
22″ × 30″, ca. 1974

the *Observer Colour Supplement* on naive artists (the magazine had a front cover by James Lloyd), he decided to send us his work which he felt was in the same category, despite an art school training. He said he attributed the work to his father because he thought we would not accept work by an artist with an academic background. After receiving a favourable reply from us, his wife Alice suggested to him that it was rather immoral to build up a false reputation in this way, and so the truth emerged. Ironically, his father, when he heard about John's pretence decided that perhaps he could paint and did produce some paintings which were "very naive," according to Patrick, but "not very good . . ."

As early as December 1967, Patrick had an exhibition of thirty paintings at Portal. Compared with his later work, the finish was crude, but they had enormous charm—a taboo word in the art sense but applicable, accurate and unashamed when applied to Patrick. The subjects all had a strong nineteenth-century flavour. The animals looked somewhat moth–eaten and stuffed, and his soldiers were in full highland dress, sometimes with a rustic background, all very bright and colourful. The paintings were very much enjoyed by collectors and critics alike. Patrick was a great success and this allowed him to give up his job in the carpet factory to start painting full time.

He painted quickly, and the quality of his work improved. He had his second exhibition a year later, of paintings that were fuller and even more imaginative. There were angels and clowns in Victorian settings, as well as portraits of his grandparents. Unlike his own working class family, these were portraits of the middle class. The children in his pictures wear long dresses over layer upon layer of petticoats and are as asexual as the Victorian wax dolls. These cumbersome, rather inelegant children are frequently surrounded by a rather sinister toy world of jack-in-the-boxes, hoops and tops, furry animals or roaring beasts. Young musicians, usually black, strumming banjos are often included—shades of the early minstrel shows. These musical paintings include a few painted guitars and banjos which Patrick had collected. They are particularly beautiful objects and were quickly bought by musicians. Patrick was friendly with the folk singer, Donovan, who used one of his paintings for the album "HMS Donovan." He collaborated in Hollywood on the film, *An Old Fashioned Picture Book*, a combination of animation and live action which was shown on U.S. television and at the Los Angeles County Museum, narrowly missing an Academy Award nomination.

Patrick's work became popular with pop personalities and some of his best work appeared in 1969 in Alan Aldridge's *Beatles Illustrated Lyrics* and the *Daily Telegraph Colour Supplement* (October 1969). He also did the cover for a Humblebums album (Transatlantic records, 1969). Patrick's paintings were exhibited in several international exhibitions—the second triennial of Insitic art in Bratislava in 1969, and the International Exhibition of Naive Art, Lugano, Switzerland in 1969—and he appears in Otto Bihalji-Merin's book, *Modern Primitives*, published by Thames and Hudson, 1972. Patrick's paintings have been bought by the Contemporary Arts Society of Great Britain, the Surrey Education Committee, the Lobel Gallery, Stockholm, the Friesner Art Institute, New York, the Fassler Collection in Connecticut, and were in the collection of the late Olga Deterding, London.

PATRICK
Luvers.
Water color, 3″ × 5″

189

However, as surprisingly as he had begun, and despite his tremendous success (four Portal exhibitions), Patrick virtually gave up painting in the mid-seventies, since which time he has only undertaken a handful of commissions and some huge murals for a Glasgow community housing project. He felt that he had something to write as well as paint. The result was *The Slab Boys*, a successful play which won him the London Evening Standard Playwright Award in 1979. He has not been a frequent visitor to the gallery but during the summer of 1981 he paid us a friendly call during which time he discussed his re-entry into the art world. He remained non-committal, but we think we shall be seeing some new Patricks in the not too distant future.

XXIX

Guy Taplin

Guy Taplin carves what Americans call decoys, but which I prefer to call wildlife wood sculptures. Decoys are functional objects, made to deceive their fellow species. Taplin's birds do no such thing—they are made with some artistic license to attract Homo sapiens.

Guy was born in the East End of London in 1939 and, like a lot of British kids in the fifties, he left school at 15 to take a job. He worked first with the General Post Office as a messenger boy, complete with red bicycle, then in the army for two years of national service in Cyprus. He hated every moment. A multitude of jobs followed this, as meat porter, ladies' hairdresser, truck driver, life guard, street vendor, cook, gardener, clerk, designer of fashion accessories and finally, bird keeper.

Like many self-taught artists, Guy Taplin has been an itinerant worker. I think he holds a record among our artists for a variety of occupations, but it was during his last job that his real vocation suddenly came to him. As keeper of wild fowl in London's Regents Park, he spent several hours of the day in a small hut on an island in the lake. This lake teems with many species of ducks, swans and geese. Guy's interest became intense and he studied them closely, reading all he could at the local library on various water fowl and other birds, before deciding to attempt a carving. He began with old pieces of wood picked up along the shore of the Thames. He preferred carving to painting or drawing, as the three–dimensional results gave him greater pleasure and he loved the feel of weathered wood. Guy claims he finds his materials in the strangest places, from the banks of the Thames to the Essex marshes and beaches where he

finds marvellous pieces of driftwood. He even raids "skips" and builders' yards, for old nails, washers and pieces of iron. Each bird is usually set on an object, such as a tree stump, often made out of an old telegraph pole, or perched on an old piece of iron railing. He recently brought us a heron carved from the mast of an old Thames barge and pieces of drift wood. Full-sized, painted swans are made of old railway sleepers and their beaks are painted with a home-ground yellow-orange paint. He works directly from a pencilled outline on the wood to the finished carving. For heavy bricks, he uses a handsaw and often laminates with glue when necessary. The work has a primitive quality and, as previously mentioned, is often mistaken for an eighteenth or nineteenth century wooden decoy, but Taplin has never consciously attempted to copy these. The breadth of his

GUY TAPLIN
Swan.
Carved and painted wood, 1980

range within the world of wild fowl is not only restricted to ducks; he also carves birds—gulls in particular—and even a humble robin, perched on a garden spade. His immense patience and deep study of these feathered creatures has been allied to his study of Zen Buddhism, which has had a very profound influence on his life.

Guy used to work in a loft/studio overlooking the Thames but now, recently married, he lives and works in a cottage near his beloved Essex estuary. Although he does not exhibit regularly, he did have a Portal exhibition in 1979. Many of his sculptures are in American folk art collections, notably those of Jackie Onassis and film director Mike Nichols. My favourite piece is a black rook which peeps through a jungle of plants in my own apartment.

GUY TAPLIN
Crow.
Carved and painted wood, 1981

X X X

James McNaught

There is a surprising element which predominates among the work of the five Scottish artists featured in this book; a kind of "phantom" chain which links their work. The subject matter of these painters has something in common, although the individual artists are scarcely aware of each other, except Hall and Fawcett, and they certainly had not seen each other's work until their own style had become well established. This seems to be when the artistic poltergeist appears and injects a "wee Scots hobgoblin" into their fantastic and eccentric paintings. This school of Scottish painters leads the viewer into marvellous fantasy worlds, inhabited by strange, idiosyncratic characters.

James McNaught is one of these artists. Born in Glasgow in 1948, he is the only son of parents who were carpet designers. His parents were very interested in the arts and James' earliest memory of a painting is a Picasso work of a lady whom he firmly believed to be his mother. The family lived in a dreary Glasgow tenement in which he remembers sitting at a table bespattered with plaster which had fallen from the crumbling ceiling, and unconcernedly painting pictures of steam ships. Also, he recalls the only subjects he really enjoyed in school were drawing and painting, hence his remaining bottom of the class for most of his scholastic career. Finally in 1966, without any qualifications, he wangled his way into art school so that he could continue with his painting for a few more years, before having to look for a job. He enjoyed his time there, although he was conscious of the poor quality of the tuition and bad

work that most of the students were doing. In fact, he was exceptional, in that he knew about painting when he started at college, more than most of the students did when they left it!

Finally, he left in 1970 to work in a hotel as a porter, cum waiter, whilst living in a caravan nearby and as he says, "ruining his cache of painting ideas." His desire to continue with his painting resulted in his finding a job as an uncertified teacher. He was placed in front of a class

JAMES McNAUGHT
*Daniel in
the Lion's Den.*
Gouache/paper,
12″ × 14″, 1979

195

James McNaught
Impresario.
Gouache/paper

of fifteen year old girls whom he says were lovely to look at, but were unbelievably aggressive to work with. He struggled, and, with regained confidence in his work, filled all his spare time with painting. He took a job as a warder in a hostel at Culzean Castle, a sombre, mouldy old ruin he describes as a "fly cemetery"; the first time he ran a bath, thousands of these flies appeared floating in the water and he had to leave the water

JAMES McNAUGHT
The Wedding Guest.
Gouache/paper,
10″ × 11″, 1979

running for days to get rid of them. Even then, there was always the odd wing, leg or body floating about!

James then alternated between odd jobs as wardens of other dreary establishments and teaching in local schools. He was forever painting when he should have been teaching, thus, most of his work is small and done in gouache—easily hidden. In 1973, on one of these boring jobs, all he could do safely was doodle with a ballpoint pen, and it was out of this phase that his present style of fantasy began to emerge. These slightly obscene drawings, often done on the inside covers of school jotters, were important in the development of his future work and had a Klee-like quality. They were how he saw events that happened around him.

His home-life at this time had still not improved, as the flat he was sharing with a friend was so damp that they both had to wear overcoats and keep a fire burning throughout the summer. He decided to take off, and visited Amsterdam, where he was amazed to find as many as eighty galleries in a city that was the same size as Glasgow, which has about 6. Most of these galleries were selling appalling paintings at high prices. His work was accepted by the Gallerie Petit, where he had his first exhibition. From Holland he travelled all over Europe, as far as Turkey, working his way around, selling an odd painting. In 1977, he met a German girl with whom he has settled in Scotland. Of course, as soon as McNaught and Portal came together in 1978, we both knew that it was an inevitable combination. These small and very powerful paintings are like odd passages from Alfred Jarry, Beckett or Ionesco. Look carefully into each one. Several are already in the United States and we are looking forward to a one-man exhibition in 1982.

X X X I

Perle Hessing

Although Perle Hessing was born in the small Polish town of Zaleszy, formerly part of the Austro-Hungarian Empire, she and her husband, Siegfried, settled in London many years ago after wandering around the world in search of a home. They are now both British subjects, and thus, she qualifies for inclusion in this book as a British self-taught painter. Perle and Siegfried have one son, Leonard, who also lives in London and is an architect.

As a child, Perle was strangely influenced by her father, a printer and bookbinder. He filled her mind with a complex and detailed knowledge of Jewish mysticism and legend, as revealed in the Bible, the Sacred Scrolls of the Talmud, and the even more secret Cabala. These stories, allied to a very vivid imagination, remain crystal clear in Perle's mind up to the present day.

In 1938, the Hessings' life became a nightmare when Austria succumbed to the Nazis. Perle will not discuss the details of this horrendous period which still remains too painful to think about. The family, although separated, did survive the holocaust and after wandering through many countries penniless, unable to communicate, Perle reached Cyprus where, after an eighteen month internment, she was allowed to go to Israel. After one year in Israel she was reunited with her son, then studying in Paris, and together they emigrated to Australia where they were later joined by Siegfried and lived for over twenty years. The Australian climate was detrimental to Perle's somewhat delicate constitution

PERLE HESSING
Homage to Spinoza.
Oil/canvas, 28″ × 24″,
1977

and during the early sixties she visited Europe and decided to settle in London. She was encouraged by her son to take up painting seriously. In Australia she had been seized by the urge to paint and it was her strange childhood memories that were awakened. In a similar way to Isaac Bashevis Singer, the weird and wonderful storyteller, Perle Hessing wanted to tell these mysterious Jewish beliefs and stories told to her by her father so many years before, but in picture form. Her simple, naive imagery is easy to understand, her colours are full and sensuous, like Jewish cooking. She works like an illustrator, employing a narrative style reminiscent of medieval manuscripts or Ethiopian paintings on goat-skin, each section flowing into the next, often using a central character, as if the painting itself is secondary to the story. Perle works slowly and produces pictures which are like a Seder feast. There are terrible monsters, like the awe inspiring "Golem" of Prague, which pop in and out with a mystical, Chagall-like quality. The phantoms float over ancient Jewish graveyards which awake long-forgotten fears. Biblical stories abound and look as if they are from the pages of ancient Haggaddahs. Traditional Jewish festivals, like the Kol Nidre, take place in a small Polish cottage with the resplendent ancient ram's horn, the shofar, and a Menorah with three candles blazing. The small family, attired in religious Jewish regalia, are observed by a passing angel peering through the window. Her narratives stretch from biblical to almost modern times. Very occasionally she has forced herself to paint her most painful memories in order to help future generations see the futility of persecution and war. One of these is

PERLE HESSING
The Dybbuk.
Oil/canvas, 40″ × 30″
1968

entitled *Children of Terzin on the Way to Auschwitz* and hangs in the Prague State Museum.

In Australia, Perle has had one-man shows at the Rudi Kamen Gallery in Sydney, the Brian Johnson Gallery in Brisbane and Macquarie Gallery in Canberra, and her paintings hang in several Australian museums. Perle had a full exhibition at Portal Gallery in 1974, and each year since then has been represented in our Christmas show, which usually features a biblical theme.

In 1977, Perle painted an astonishing life story picture of the philosopher Spinoza, which included all the focal points of his life, his ambitions, even his dreams. This complex and full painting was reproduced as the frontispiece of her husband's book *Speculum Spinoanum*, compiled to celebrate the tercentenary of Spinoza that year.

opposite:
PERLE HESSING
Kol Nidre.
Oil/canvas, 30″ × 26″, 1973

PERLE HESSING
The Golem.
Oil/canvas, 36″ × 30″, 1964

PERLE HESSING
Cane and Abel.

XXXII

Rosemary Fawcett

Although born in Yorkshire, England in 1947, Rosemary Fawcett is one of the select group of Scottish artists mentioned in this book. From early childhood she lived in the Scottish border country, better known in a certain popular song as the "lowlands." This rugged and wild country-side, which is divided by Hadrian's wall, is in parts one of the remotest and bleakest parts of Britain, and it is this area which had provided inspiration for the landscapes which form the background in many of Rosemary's paintings. Most of Rosemary's adult life has been spent in the Glasgow area, but these brutal landscapes still glow in her memory.

Her early training as a textile designer led her to become an artist. Within her paintings the same esoteric qualities emerged as in all the work by this small school of Scottish artists—shades of the unmentionable, "mad" Scottish poet, William McGonagall, a name which does not seem to be as acceptable in Scotland as it is in England. Perhaps he is something of a worn-out joke as far as the Scots are concerned—rather like the Loch Ness Monster. Nevertheless, monsters seem to proliferate in Rosemary Fawcett's work. She paints in gouache, and her colours, which are never brash, have something of a faded, antique quality about them. Her monsters are not ferocious but friendly, if somewhat melancholy (which is understandable looking at their rather strange surroundings). These animals and birds are recognisable, but in a quite peculiar way they seem to be slightly larger than life. Some, like *Ludwig's Swan*, are described by Rosemary as examples of "romantic realism," an apt description which

combines her own strange fantasies and the influence of the northern European painters of the 14th and 15th centuries which he admires so much.

The titles from her first Portal show in 1979 read like an ancient manuscript; *A Centaur Serenades Marcissus, St. Jerome in the Wilderness, Mermaid with Seahorse,* and *Tristan and Isolde leaving Ireland* are among the strangest and most romantic. This, her first London exhibition, was noticed by publishers, Jonathan Cape, who were planning a book with the international author, Roald Dahl, using the somewhat dramatic title of *Dirty Beasts*. Rosemary Fawcett was the obvious choice to paint this series of beasts to accompany Dahl's text and the book is due for publication in early 1982.

ROSEMARY FAWCETT
Ludwig's Swan.
Gouache/paper, 12″ × 17″,
1978

ROSEMARY FAWCETT
Chicken.
Gouache/paper, 7″ × 7″, 1978

X X X I I I
Reg Cartwright

That the surname Cartwright evokes an image of rural England in the late nineteenth century is particularly appropriate, as Reginald Cartwright paints intuitive "portraits" of this peaceful era.

Reg was born in almost the geographical centre of England, Leicestershire, in 1938. After somewhat unmemorable school days at the Gateway Boys' School, he decided to embark on a musical career as he derived most pleasure and distinction at school from playing the trumpet. These plans were thwarted when he was conscripted into the army for a two year spell in Her Majesty's Forces. Although he continued playing for a military band à la Douanier Rousseau, and had not given up his ambition to become a professional musician when he left the army, a stronger ambition to become an artist began to emerge. While still playing trumpet in local dance bands and orchestras he managed to gratify his artistic leanings at the time by doing posters advertising the dances or concerts that he appeared in.

Around 1969, Reg became more involved with his painting and, since the early seventies, has been a full time artist. He found his models all around him—country people, farm workers, nurserymen, vicars, old age pensioners, local teachers, trades people, retired civil servnts, postmen and the village "bobby" are all represented in Cartwright's paintings. He painted portraits of people going about their daily lives with the background of the English village ever present. Representing a bygone era which still exists alongside the modern space age cities, the paintings are

Reg Cartwright
The Garden.
Oil/canvas

composed with absolute precision and clarity. With a somewhat naive framework, the artist is visually aware of all these people who make up the small village community in Leicestershire in which he still lives. Each village has a social structure and each of the inhabitants makes sure it is precisely adhered to. Reg very accurately portrays this structure within his paintings. Nobody ever wears anything but the almost traditional uniform they are meant to wear, faithfully preserved by him in his unwavering, flat, clear finish.

Most of Cartwright's paintings are large, some up to five feet square. Sometimes one feels one is looking through the window of a cottage at a local scenario.

Between 1970 and 1980, Cartwright has had four one-man shows at Portal and has also exhibited at the King Street Gallery and in Windsor, where Windsor and Eton published a limited edition print of one of his paintings.

In 1979 London's Hutchinson book publishers published Reg's first book of paintings, *Mr Potter's Pigeon*, for which a text was written by a young friend of his, Patrick Kinmouth. The book has become a best seller and although suitable for all ages, has won the coveted children's book prize, the Mother Goose Award, for the most exciting newcomer to children's book illustration. A new book is currently being prepared by Reg and we look forward to holding an exhibition in conjunction with its publication. During recent years, a group of British West country painters led by the international artist Peter Blake have called themselves the "Brotherhood of Ruralists." Cartwright lives far away from them but had he lived nearby he would be a perfect candidate, as the title "ruralist" describes his work perfectly.

REG CARTWRIGHT
At the Doorway.
Oil/Canvas

XXXIV

James Grainger

Now twenty-five years of age and living in Kent with his wife and daughter, James Grainger is the son of an eminent archaeologist and was reared in a somewhat academic background. As soon as his parents allowed him to grab a pencil, the kitchen table became his easel. It soon became obvious that young James was no mere childish scribbler. As early as his seventh year, his ambition was to become an artist, and, encouraged by his parents with the birthday present of a "junior oil paint set," he began his career seriously by copying comic book characters from the popular English *Beano*. One such portrait he remembers was of "Dennis the Menace," a figure of national importance in juvenile circles.

At the age of ten, James achieved what most artists wait several decades for—a chance to exhibit his work at a local art exhibition. He was offered five shillings for his masterpiece, *Fruit Still Life*, but did not succumb to the temptation and personally anounced it as not for sale.

As a teenager, his passion for painting did not subside and, despite a series of local jobs which he was forced to take, he continued painting and returned to his original medium of pencil drawing. He worked in this media exclusively for several years, drawing dreamy landscapes in a very mature style with such unlikely titles as, *Why Don't You Eat Carrots?*

After viewing the great old masters, Goya, Breugel and Bosch, whilst travelling in Spain and Portugal, he regained his enthusiasm for oils. His ambition to improve his technique in oils was wholly inspired by these great allegorical masterpieces. Gradually his own compositions changed,

JAMES GRAINGER
Clergy Tossing.
Oil/canvas, 1981

taking more realistic forms. James' grandfather, who he considers the ultimate model, began to appear in each painting. Together with his ambition, the size of his paintings grew until, in 1974, he started on a huge canvas which took him two years to complete. Sadly, the hazards of living in a small flat at the time made storage a major problem, and, as he says, "It was inevitable that a foot would find its way through the canvas." His paintings gradually became a more manageable size and his very finely executed subject matter became an attractive blend of surrealistic humour and reality. He loves to paint anything typically British and of course slightly eccentric, using colours from the classic British landscape school. In 1977, the year that Portal accepted his work as our youngest artist, he was granted the honour of exhibiting in the Royal Academy Summer Exhibition. Since then, he has appeared annually at this premier British art event and has also exhibited regularly with Portal. At the moment, he

JAMES GRAINGER
Pig Racing at the Vicarage.
Oil/canvas, 11″ × 17″, 1981

opposite:
JAMES GRAINGER
*In Search of
the Greak Auk.*
Oil/canvas, 1981

is working on a series of paintings of British vicars which should be completed late in 1982. "My main aim is to produce humourous pictures and a sure sign of success is a laugh from the mother-in-law."

X X X V

Elizabeth Hopkin

Clearly an exception to the legion of faux-naives creating their paintings in Europe, Yugoslavia and Haiti, Elizabeth Hopkin is a rarity, a genuine naive artist. Her work remains distinct from the cruder primitive artist's, but can also be labelled self-taught. Despite her personal sophistication, her paintings contain a distinctly childlike innocence which most people automatically associate with the naive artist. Born in the upper Swansea valley, Elizabeth Hopkin is one of the few Welsh self-taught artists that we exhibit. I am particularly fond of Wales, a mysterious and ancient civilisation of strange beauty. This small, often misunderstood country is not to be confused with neighbouring England. It is relatively inaccessible in parts, but a visit is well worth the effort.

Elizabeth is a trim and pretty lady who confesses to be in her mid-fifties, appears to be in her forties but is suspected to be in her early sixties. She has four grandchildren at school. One of her daughters, Mary Hopkin, is the popular vocalist who was discovered by the Beatles during the late sixties.

Elizabeth's father was a professional photographer of national repute who captured the beautiful and sombre scenic splendour of the Welsh mining valleys and villages. Elizabeth was rather more interested in the local characters, honest miners and the parochial village life, and as a hobby she began sketching these scenes. It was during the thirties and forties that a small colony of European artists gathered in this area. They admired its natural beauty and were attracted by its traditions. Elizabeth had married an architect and the couple made friends with some of these

ELIZABETH HOPKIN
*Daniel in
the Lion's Den.*
Water color, 21″ × 15″

artists; this no doubt triggered off her desire to paint. She tried her hand at watercolours, found she enjoyed herself and pleased her family, so she continued to paint. Her goal initially was to interest the children and she depicted her childhood memories of the village community in which she lived—all the big occasions in a mining community like the collier's fete, local elections, funerals and the opening of the first cinema, picnics, parties, carnivals, floods, the "sweetie" shops where the kids congregated, Christmas scenes and rainy days on top of the omnibus. All these events painted with great care are a unique chronicle of life within this small Welsh village community, seen through the innocent eyes of a child but executed with the formal composition of an adult. It is the imaginative

ELIZABETH HOPKIN
Birth of a Nation.
Water color, 15″ × 21″,
1979

colours and oversize figures which combine to give Hopkin's work a curious charm of its own.

Today, most of the pits have closed and the tiny villages are beginning to lose much of their isolation, due to nearby motorways. Elizabeth has ceased to sketch her local environment and has introduced a new and slightly crazy fantasy into her work. These recent paintings are not as sweet as her early work but are emerging with a new crispness and humour. *Birth of a Nation*—memories of a first movie visit—shows hundreds of babies emerging from the cinema, a strange and arresting painting. *Daniel in the Lion's Den* is left over from her own Sunday school days and translated into a dream. Her colours have become muted in comparison to her earlier work and I think they benefit much from this change.

Elizabeth Hopkin had her successful first exhibition with us in 1976 and has been a regular exhibiter since then. She and her husband continue to live and work in their beautiful Welsh valley.

XXXVI

Ronnie Copas

Now in his early forties, Ronnie Copas was born in the London borough of Lambeth and, like his fellow artist John Allin, was raised in the East End during the war years. Though their backgrounds are similar, Copas and Allin have opposing artistic styles. One might say that they span the Portal spectrum; both artists are self-taught but, where Allin's work leans towards the primitive, Copas veers towards the academic, where Allin has a purely factual style Copas' style is a combination of reality and imagination.

Copas began to paint seriously at the age of sixteen. His ambition was to attend art school but finances were inadequate and he had to forgo this ambition to help support the family. Now, twenty-five years later, Copas declares that not going to art school was the best thing that could have happened to him as an artist. Having left school at the age of thirteen myself, I concur with him. To teach oneself a subject, one must have a genuinely strong desire to learn and, consequently, one emerges with a more thorough knowledge of that subject.

It was a few years, however, before Copas discovered his natural style. He describes his own work of the early sixties as somewhat loosely impressionistic although the work was good enough to sell reasonably well locally. He was married and living in Chelsea and at this time he supplemented his work as an artist with work as a theatrical scene painter and a graphic designer. He feels these outside jobs actually enhanced his

work as an artist, helping him to discover techniques and short cuts applicable to his paintings.

In 1969 Ronnie Copas and his wife decided to leave London for what was, in comparison, a primitive community at the tip of England overlooking the Atlantic Ocean in Cornwall. They found a tiny cottage on St. Michael's Mount, an offshore island inhabited mainly by fisherman and a community of nuns—a sharp contrast to Chelsea. Accepted by this small but friendly community, Ronnie became an integral part by taking a job as a boatman, ferrying visitors between St. Michael's Mount and the mainland. He enjoyed this tough, manual job and, although the physical effort of rowing a heavy boat often exhausted him, he began to realise that this encounter with the elements was providing him with a new dimension as an artist although he had less time to paint. The strength of

RONNIE COPAS
Grace Over Starry Gazy Pie.
Egg tempera, 21″ × 14″, 1977

RONNIE COPAS
*Nuns Aboard
the Viking Hobbler.*
Egg tempera, 22″ × 16″

his new environment seeped into his work—the raw, powerful ocean off the Cornish coastline, the treacherous sands, the weatherbeaten fishermen and their womenfolk, the nuns from the convent on the Mount and, above all, the local lifeboatmen fighting against nature in an effort to save a sinking fishing boat. He worked at this new sophisticated yet primitive style using a mixture of egg tempera with resin oil, a technique developed by fifteenth century Florentine artists, which requires an elaborate and lengthy preparation and skill in application. He uses a beeswax finish, and, although the paint he applies has a matte finish, the colours are deep, lustrous and alive. Copas' ocean is a luminous green, similar to that of Alfred Wallis, the great primitive painter who lived all his life in the same part of Cornwall. Not all of Ronnie's work is connected with the sea; new and powerful figures emerge in a style that has developed reminiscently of the finest British twentieth-century artists such as the late Sir Stanley Spencer. These elongated and somewhat distorted figures are surrounded by superbly detailed backgrounds and these paintings exude a religious atmosphere. In *Star Gazy Pie* we see what appears to be an eighteenth or nineteenth-century interior, but is a present day Cornish fisherman's cottage with the family and the local vicar offering their thanks to the Lord for the delicious home-cooked delicacy they are about to consume for Sunday dinner. A bold and moving painting with an obvious spiritual content, it was this marvellous painting that we selected for the catalogue of his first exhibition in 1976. It is no doubt Ronnie Copas' unusual technique that gives these works such an immediately recognisable image. His subjects are authentic and often delve into Cornish tradition and language—the famous floral dancers and the hobbler, a local name for a special wooden raw boat, and the Lug Seekers appear amongst his titles. Within this imagery appear many strange, distorted folk who are dancing madly through the small, winding, village streets, accompanied by an out-of-tune band, reminiscent of medieval tapestry. *The Chess Players*, a brilliant composition, depicts two young men wearing black and white check shirts, leaning on a chessboard into which they merge. The scene takes place in a strange garden with mysterious figures disappearing over the brick walls. Copas' paintings vary from small gems to a double triptych, six by five feet, which hangs in St Andrew's Church, Pencoys, in Cornwall. A recent canvas entitled *St Francis and the Wildfowl* was commissioned by Sir Peter Scott and the Wildfowl Trust, and hangs at their headquarters in Slimbridge, Hampshire.

RONNIE COPAS
The Chess Players.
Egg tempera,
29″ × 20″, 1978

opposite:
RONNIE COPAS
*St. Francis and
the Wildfowl.*
Resin oil/canvas,
72″ × 56″, 1980

224

Before he exhibited at the Portal Gallery, Copas contributed works to the Victor Passmore Gallery, Newlyn, Cornwall, and Penwith Society, St Ives, Cornwall. Both of these galleries are considered to be among the most important British provincial art galleries and have examples of some of Britain's leading artists who have lived in the area since the 1920s. Sometime ago Lionel Levy and I discussed the possibility of commissioning an Haggadah by a contemporary artist, and Ronnie Copas was the obvious choice. It was only on approaching Copas that we discovered that he is in fact partly Jewish. He has a keen interest in Jewish folklore and was, consequently, familiar with the Haggadah and its colourful Passover stories, concerning the Children of Israel. Copas started work on this project about two years ago and hopes to complete it during 1982/3, when we will be exhibiting the paintings. The subject is perhaps rather curiously suited to his style.

RONNIE COPAS
The Furry,
or Floral Dance.
Egg tempera, 1978

XXXVII

Irvine Peacock

Thirty-three year old Irvine Peacock hails from the northern steel town of Middlesborough, where he attended the local high school and admits to taking art class to avoid playing rugby. He so enjoyed art classes that he took a pre-diploma course at the local college between 1964–1966, a happy period for him. This curriculum consisted of drawing and painting from life in a conventional manner. However, his somewhat lackadaisical attitude was shaken when he decided to follow through with a three-year course at the Sheffield School of Art. He eventually left this establishment, completely disillusioned with the attitudes of the British art school establishments, about which he comments: "They lack the judgement to select students on the basis of their work. They rely on examination passes in subjects probably unrelated while the most talented person with qualification is rejected. Why are exams necessary in order to 'teach' fine arts courses in England? They are just an expensive way of producing teachers, or were. Even when I did the course, it was terrible. The only advice I was given was to look in the Studio International magazine for ideas. The staff favoured large 'cool' paintings and non-figurative reliefs, often done with masking tape. The only figurative paintings accorded any respect were either huge paintings of baked beans, or beach-type scenes in the David Hockney style. Any kind of personal vision was discouraged. Art was seen as the activity of an informed elite and the artist was like a nuclear physicist holding specialised knowledge, producing theories,

being involved in activities, most of which appeared as gibberish to the layman, the man in the street, who in fact was paying the taxes to pay for the whole thing.

"This is just a reworking of the artist as genius theme which is another way of isolating the working class from their potential as producers and 'appreciators' of art. Also, this is exactly the role of the British Arts Council, except in their case it is bare-faced nepotism, where the same small group of people either sit on the panel or receive the awards. They actually take turns (see *Art Monthly*, September 1981) and the same 'old pals' blatantly exhibit each other's work at public galleries."

IRVINE PEACOCK
The Mathematician.
Oil/board, 11″ × 15″, 1981

IRVINE PEACOCK
Jonah and the Whale.
Oil/board, 1979

In 1970, Peacock, now disillusioned and somewhat angry, attended the controversial Hornsey Art College to gain a certificate in teaching which allowed him work as an art therapist in the psychiatric units of various hospitals. This access to the work of schizophrenic patients triggered an interest, which has continued to the present day, in Jung's (and other contemporaries') writings, especially the theories of the collective unconscious and myth. This led directly to his interest, like Kit Williams', in alchemy, symbolism, iconography, totem and magic. Peacock, his wife Diane, and their two boys, isolated themselves in the wilds of the sparsely populated, flat county of Norfolk. Living in a small flint cottage, he gradually developed his now very recognisable painting technique, doing everything by hand, even grinding his own pigments. His finely detailed and beautifully coloured work shows almost a reinvention of mythology in which humans become animals, animals become birds, birds become fish and fish become humans.

Irvine Peacock is an excellent example of our paradoxical, self-taught

230

IRVINE PEACOCK
Jester. Oil/board,
15″ × 10″, 1981

artist. After learning all he could in several colleges, he felt he knew nothing about painting and started to teach himself the real thing. I feel justified in quoting Peacock at greater length than any other Portal painter, as I am in total accord with his opinions on art education in Britain. Thank goodness for the overseas visitors and collectors who appreciate our paintings and who will be looking at a full exhibition of Irvine Peacock's extraordinary paintings towards the end of 1982.

XXXVIII

Reginald Pepper

Reginald Pepper is Portal's "mystery" painter. Some few years back, a rather lovely lady appeared at the gallery with a parcel of very strange, somewhat crudely prepared paintings on unsymmetrical pieces of hardboard, finished in glossy enamel with a primitive flavour. They were all domestic scenes, but with a difference. The figures were portrayed with heavy cumbersome bodies and pea-sized heads and were haphazardly scattered about the rather mundane interiors, but the finished effect was quite riveting. As if by some kind of coincidence the compositions seemed to fit into place, almost in an academic way. Each painting was as complete and fascinating as an Alfred Wallis, but completed with detail and, when one got used to the disturbing pea-heads, they became particularly interesting paintings of obvious quality. The lady had very little to tell us about the artist. His name was Pepper. He appeared to be in his mid-fifties and lived very quietly with his widowed mother in a small town in Wiltshire. The lady lived not far away, with her family, in an old country house where there are several traditional paintings on the walls. A cleaning woman who worked for her, mentioned that she knew of a "funny" man in the village whom she often saw through the windows of his cottage, painting at a table. One day she asked the man's mother, whom she knew by sight, if her son was an artist. She learned that he was, but he did not like showing his paintings to strangers.

A few days later, the old widow brought two of her son's paintings, in her shopping bag, to the village shop, where she proudly showed them to

her acquaintance, who in due course mentioned them to her employer. Fortunately, this lady was curious, so the old widow was eventually persuaded by the cleaning woman to show her son's paintings to the "posh" lady who lived in the big house. The lovely lady felt that these peculiar pictures had a special quality and, having heard of us, brought them to the Gallery. It appeared that Reginald Pepper did odd labouring jobs locally and had never been too bright or sociable. He just sat at home painting whenever he was free. When or how he started painting is unknown, as his mother does not seem to have been interested enough to

REGINALD PEPPER
Chickens. Oil/board,
11″ × 14″, 1982

remember. She did, however, agree to sell a few of Reggie's paintings as "the money would come in very handy." To this day, we have had no direct contact with Reg Pepper. About twice a year the lovely lady appears with five or six paintings, and these reasonably priced pictures are usually snapped up by collectors. We don't think that we will ever get enough paintings together for a Pepper exhibition, or that we will ever learn any more about him, or that he knows anything about us. Even the lovely lady enjoys the mystery and cashes our cheques, handing over the money to her cleaner, who, in turn, hands it to the widow, who always writes a little note in return which reads:

REGINALD PEPPER
In the Bath. Oil/board,
14″ × 18″, 1981

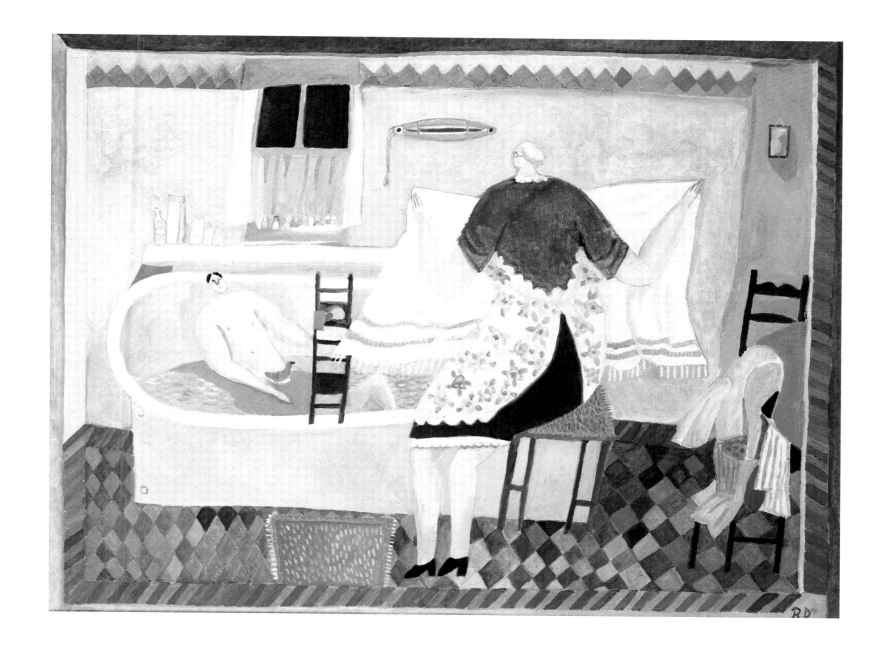

Dear Mum,

Thank you for the money for my son and me for the paintings.

Mrs. B. Pepper

Surprise! surprise! About three weeks after writing this Reginald Pepper story, based on the scanty information gathered from the lovely lady, I had a call from a journalist on the London *Sunday Times* informing me that we were under a misapprehension about one of our primitive artists, and that "Mr. Pepper" was the nom de plume of an academic artist who painted and exhibited works in two completely different styles. At almost the same time, a gentleman who introduced himself as the lovely lady's husband, came into the gallery and "confessed" on behalf of his wife, that she had actually painted all the "Reginald Peppers," but felt too embarrassed to tell us personally. Much to her relief, our attitude was in no way hostile, so she relaxed and called us to explain her reasons for the charade. After a successful exhibition of her own work in London during 1973, she decided that her pictures lacked bite and colour and were too tonal. It was then that she began thinking more about primitive painting. She felt she had learned more from the primitives than from her ten years at art school, so she invented her own primitive to release herself from the absurd academic rules of perspective, etc. She selected for her dual personality, a man who sounded right for the part, far away from her own world but at the same time accessible. She decided that her paintings would not be acceptable to the art world if she used her own name and she might damage her reputation, so Reginald Pepper was born, and she found a new success through him, plus an immense amount of enjoyment and freedom in composing the paintings. A highly selective team of Britain's top art experts chose Reginald Pepper's work to hang in the Royal Academy's Summer Exhibition in 1975, but prior to this, she had also sold Pepper's works to another London gallery. Francis Spalding, a critic writing in the magazine *Arts Review*, said of Pepper, "He evokes a personal world while other artists merely flaunt a primitive language for personal gain."

On Sunday, December 6th, 1981 the *Sunday Times* printed an in-depth articled entitled "The Bogus Life of a Primitive Artist," a somewhat sensational article, hastily put together by an ill-informed journalist, full of inaccuracies and with an obvious lack of knowledge of

what primitive art is all about. My own comments were included with a somewhat biased slant. In part, my quote was: "We would continue to take and show the Pepper paintings . . . It doesn't make any difference to us who painted the pictures, it is the quality that counts, not the personality of the painter. We still like the paintings. They are excellent."

A quote from the lady artist says, "If anybody buys a picture for the sake of the story behind it, for the idea that it's quaint and charming, because it's painted by an idiot in Swindon rather than for its own merits—well so much the worse for them."

REGINALD PEPPER
*Auntie May
at Sunday Tea.*
11" × 14", 1982

Following this article, we sold all the remaining Peppers to enthusiastic and discerning collectors. The artist has promised to continue as Reginald Pepper with the possibility of a one-man show in a year or two. We still continue to have faith in our own judgement of what merits a good painting and to hell with the stick-on labels.

XXXIX

C. W. Brown

Early in 1982, I received a letter from Peter Vigurs, the Keeper of Fine Art at the City Museum and Art Gallery in Stoke–on–Trent, Staffordshire. This exciting new museum complex had been very recently completed and was already regarded as one of the finest contemporary museums in Britain. Vigurs' letter enclosed photographs of a few paintings by an intriguing primitive artist called C. W. Brown. I was immediately struck by their "alive" quality, the essential ingredient in a good primitive. On phoning Peter Vigurs, I was surprised to hear that the new gallery had inherited about 1,000 works by this local artist who had died twenty years previously and, as the gallery had an appropriate exhibition area, they were selecting about 100 to show later in the year.

On a return trip from a visit to my family in Southport, I made a detour to Stoke–on–Trent, the traditional center of British pottery and of the famous "Five Towns" immortalised in Arnold Bennett's novel. Before looking at C. W. Brown's paintings, the main purpose of my visit, Peter Vigurs gave me a conducted tour of the magnificent Staffordshire pottery collection. The work of those great potters, including Wood, Pratt and Wheildon, were my inspiration and source of interest in self-taught artists. The primitive images on these lovely plates, mugs, dishes, and Toby jugs are valid as part of an essentially British heritage. They depict incidents in the world of sport and entertainment, incidents in English life from the seventeenth to the nineteenth centuries and often, as with paintings of the period, they were used as a means of communication.

C. W. Brown's paintings came up to my expectations. Often photographs enhance a painting—for instance a coarsely painted picture loses its rough texture when reduced by photograph—but this was not the case with Brown's work. Peter Vigurs allowed me to browse through several shelves of them. Although, like many good primitives, the work was very erratic, the best paintings and ink and wash studies were marvellous, almost a potted history of the potteries (ouch!) through the eyes of a twentieth-century working man.

Charles William Brown was born in 1882 in North Staffordshire, an area where he remained for his entire life. Brown's christening at the late age of six was at Alsager's Bank Church. Keen readers will note that James Lloyd, Britain's most important primitive, was also born in Alsager. Two

C. W. BROWN
Etruria.
Ink and wash,
16″ × 23″, 1947

C. W. Brown
Me '69.
Ink and
water color,
14″ × 10″, 1951

CW Brown 1951

"ME" '69

241

C. W. BROWN
Old Rookery Pit.
Ink and wash,
10″ × 14″, 1905

such artists from such a small place is really extraordinary. Brown's father was a coal miner and the family was very poor. His meagre schooling ceased at twelve when he was hired out to a local farmer for one shilling and sixpence (about twenty cents) per week. The farmer paid him so poorly that he soon ran off to find work as a pit boy, where his finances increased dramatically to ten shillings (one dollar) per week. However, due to a tragic pit disaster, under-aged Brown was banned from pit work and had to return to the hated farmer where he remained until he was fourteen. Brown became a miner of exceptional ability. He studied, and eventually became a colliery manager. He and his wife lived for over fifty years in the same house in Etruria, close to Stoke–on–Trent. His mining career finished in 1948 when he retired at the age of sixty-six. He lived on until 1961 and from the creative point of view, these thirteen years of retirement became the most important of his life.

He was a meticulous individual and had kept a diary for many years. As a hobby, he taught himself to paint with coloured inks and water-colours, and both these activities assumed major importance during his last years. He would write constantly his memoirs of the two World Wars and of the consequent changes in lifestyle. He had preserved several pencil sketches made since his youth and it came naturally to him to paint his reminiscences. His choice of subject matter was varied. Obviously, pit scenes and tragic disasters had become an integral part of his life and, like fellow artist Jack Crabtree, the work is obviously done with a first–hand knowledge of the conditions under which the miners live and work.

The surviving sketches which Brown bequeathed to the art gallery go

C. W. BROWN
*Mining Perils—
Trapped by a Pit Fall.*
Ink and water color,
12½″ × 20″, 1951

back to 1905 and, in the earliest work, *Old Rookery Pit, Bignall End*, we see a typical pit scene of the period. Almost fifty years later, Brown was using the same medium, ink and wash, in his moving memory sketch *Mining Perils, Trapped by a Pit Fall*. A marvellously complex ink and wash dated 1947 shows the town of Etururia in all its "glory" (or as I remember it, in all its "gloom") of the immediate post-war years.

Not all of Brown's work was quite so serious. As a senior employee in the colliery, he earned a good, steady income and, throughout the twenties, thirties and forties, he and his wife and family were able to go on occasional holidays or "Wakes weeks," as they were known in the northern counties. He remembered the pleasurable trips by steamer to the Isle of Man and was able to produce ink and watercolour drawings of these occasions and other beach scenes and country landscapes.

A powerful self-portrait entitled *Me '69* is reminiscent of James Lloyd's self-portrait, striking in its direct intensity, executed in muted colours, with particularly effective detail in the sweater he wears. An excellent flower painting done in 1944 completes this short study of Brown's work.

He survived his wife by two years and continued writing and painting until the end came in 1961. Although his paintings had hardly been accepted during his lifetime, and were turned down several times by the local museums and galleries, (in 1937, *Fruit and Flowers* was bought for three guineas by the Russell Art Gallery, Hanely), in 1947, Brown told G. Bemrose, the curator of the Stoke–on–Trent Museum and Art Gallery that "the Corporation will get all my works." The old man kept his word.

C. W. Brown
The Isle of Man Ferry.
Ink and water color,
14" × 10", 1943

LIST OF ILLUSTRATIONS